ELECTING NOT TO VOTE

ELECTING NOT TO VOTE

Christian Reflections on Reasons for Not Voting

Edited by
Ted Lewis

CASCADE *Books* · Eugene, Oregon

ELECTING NOT TO VOTE
Christian Reflections on Reasons for Not Voting

Cascade Books
A Division of Wipf and Stock Publishers
199 W. 8th Ave., Suite 3
Eugene, OR 97401

www.wipfandstock.com

ISBN 13: 978-1-55635-227-0

Cataloging-in-Publication data:

Electing not to vote : Christian reflections on reasons for not voting / Edited with an introduction by Ted Lewis.

xiv + 126 p. ; 23 cm. — Includes bibliographical references.

ISBN 13: 978-1-55635-227-0

1. Voting—Religious aspects—Christianity. 2. Christianity and politics—United States. I. Lewis, Ted. II. Title.

BR516 .E444 2008

Manufactured in the U.S.A.

Dedicated to

G. Scott Becker

a contributor to this book

who died on September 13, 2007

from cancer.

He was en route to getting his PhD

at Fuller Theological Seminary.

*The grass withers, the flower fades, when the breath
of the Lord blows upon it.*

—Isaiah 40:7

*Love is the NEW doing, THE new doing, which is the meaning and
fulfillment of all 'not doing'. . . . Love does not enter into competition,
and therefore it cannot be defeated.*

—Karl Barth, from his commentary on Romans 13,
The Epistle to the Romans

Table of Contents

Introduction

Ted Lewis

Writing about legitimate reasons for not voting is not easy in our society. One feels as though he or she is trespassing into a forbidden zone of conversation or violating someone's personal space. We are socialized to think that voting, while a very public activity, is nonetheless a very private act. For years this activity was reinforced by the old voting booths, in which curtains were drawn, and voting levers were pulled with no one watching. And in the aftermath of election day, it would certainly be bad form to ask someone to reveal personal voting selections—perhaps on par with asking someone to reveal one's weight or annual income.

So we confront a cultural mind-set that applauds the freedom and privilege to vote and that resists any hint of undermining this civic practice. So strong is our notion that good citizenship implies good "votership," that the institution of voting remains too sacred, too untouchable as a topic for critical analysis. The writers of this volume, however, consider themselves in good company, especially as they reflect on the precedent set by Jesus for questioning the social and religious institutions of his day. He crossed all sorts of social boundaries, plunging into public and private sacred zones for the sake of a greater ethic, and certainly for the sake of a greater God.

This book aims to pull the voting-booth curtain back, so to speak, in order to create a new kind of freedom: specifically, a freedom for readers to ask questions that for the most part have not been welcome within the discourse of our society and of our faith communities. These questions are multiple, but a root question that stirs each of the contributors to this volume is as follows: How does Christian faith inform the way we engage the practice of voting? And more specifically, might there be legitimate, faith-based reasons for electing not to vote? To this last question, all nine authors of this book have offered a positive response, and this shared re-

ix

sponse is precisely what holds the book together. This book has no grand goal of trying to convince readers to adopt this new orientation for themselves; rather the goal of the book is to create new lines of discussion for the sake of sharper thinking and faith-inspired acting.

No matter where you stand on this issue, you cannot escape a certain question: At what point in the political course of a society would you be compelled by your own conscience not to vote? We cannot help but transport ourselves back into twentieth-century history, into countries that were shifting from democratic to dictatorial regimes. There is a good chance that we all could draw a line at some point where our faith and principles would lead us to not participate in voting. But what would our reasons be? Corrupt candidates? Corrupt election processes? Corrupt government policies? My point is that once you concede the legitimacy of not voting in certain situations, you have opened yourself up to a larger discussion about having sound reasons for voting or not voting in any situation.

Fortunately, the nine authors of the following essays do not all share the same reasons for not voting. Some authors spell out different thresholds at which they would not vote, based upon qualities of candidates or governments; others spell out a consistent stance for not voting regardless of the political state of affairs. But all of them agree that valid, compelling reasons exist for someone's choice not to vote, and these reasons are based on principled thinking and biblical teaching. The writers (all men except for one, all European American except for one Asian American and one African American) are explicitly working to frame the issues in Christian ways, but it is my hope that readers who do not share the same faith commitments will still find these essays to have useful and broader applications within the realm of ethics.

Here we face a second reason that this book is hard to write. Over the past two centuries, certain segments of American society were denied access to vote, and costly sacrifices were made both for and by these groups to obtain the right and freedom to vote. Who are we, then, to even suggest that there are solid, ethical reasons—or biblical, ecclesial reasons—for not voting, when the road to gain this privilege has been hard fought by many? Is it not almost disrespect to them to present a counterweight against the very thing that offers hope for their future? These are good questions, and the contributors of this book all sense the complexities at hand.

And yet the contributors would not have submitted their writings were it not for a set of considerations that outweighed traditional or progressive rationales for the merits of voting. Such considerations are not necessarily inviting readers to disengage from civic or political involvement. To the contrary, nearly all of the essays strongly advocate a form of active engagement beyond voting abstention, but it is a qualified engagement, an engagement that is shaped more by biblical ideals than patriotic ideals. At the same time, these essays necessarily present a sharp prophetic challenge to the way things operate in our political realm, and as I mentioned before, the authors find themselves in the company of Jesus and of the prophets of Israel and Judah.

John Roth offers five basic Anabaptist principles for a "conscientious abstention" from voting. Roth sees that such an abstention from voting may be flexible: It may be for a season of time, or it may be for the long haul. In either case, the intentional decision amounts to a heightening of the church's distinctive witness to the world.

Andy Alexis-Baker revisits the work of John Howard Yoder in order to examine the Constantinian legacy that still operates within today's politics. The unquestioned acceptance of the "state-as-savior" reinforces how voting is a sacred ritual involving a "confession of faith." The alternative to this confessional practice, following Yoder's lead, involves new ecclesial practices that reveal the church as a political body unto itself. Such a body operates under a new ethos of decision-making that rivals conventional models of decision-making.

Nekeisha Alexis-Baker, with considerable documentation from African American Christian writing, notes within the black church the rich history of alternative forms of social engagement that allowed members a significant voice in society. Alexis-Baker exposes the flaws in the commonly held myth of "voting as voice," suggesting that accepting this myth weakens a community's political imagination to find deeper, alternative engagements with the world. Alexis-Baker views the civil rights movement itself in a new light beyond the issue of voter power.

G. Scott Becker finds his dialogue within the Baptist evangelical context where the main options seem limited to pietistic withdrawal or the formation of a Christian nation. He looks to Karl Barth's engagement with the Nazi regime and at Barth's disengagement from the Communist threat as providing a better compass for Christians best speaking God's message into the world. Barth's Christology of divine humility also points the way toward voting abstention as it sheds light on the self-deification of political processes.

Michael Degan examines the classic Mennonite themes of nonresistance and kingdom theology. He provides a substantial review of North American Mennonite texts from the first half of the twentieth century—texts that deal with "God-and-Caesar" issues, and Degan links patriotic duty with Jesus's view of mammon. Participation in partisan politics compromises one's capacity to resist evil without coercion and to love one's enemy. Degan recognizes that the ultimate problem with voting has to do with "who I become in order to win."[1]

Todd David Whitmore covers a Catholic perspective on not voting, explaining the ways that a bishops' statement on "faithful citizenship" can fit with a decision not to vote for any presidential candidate rather than to vote for a "lesser evil." Whitmore specifically analyzes the stances of President Bush and Senator Kerry from the 2004 elections, and poses a guiding question: "is the distance between Catholic teaching and the candidate nearest to it greater than the distance between the candidates?"[2]

Paul Alexander, within the Pentecostal tradition, reviews the nonviolent, nonpartisan, and nonnationalistic emphases within early Pentecostal literature. Out of this study he poses a third-way option between the all-too-common polarities of political withdrawal and political abdication. His "prophetic, patriotic Pentecostal pacifism" opens up doors for Christians to be "citizens and patriots in the kingdom of God," wherein the duties of noncoercive love transcend the duties of voting.[3]

Tato Sumantri continues the development of this ecclesial theme, suggesting that the way an authentic church operates is both incoherent and irrelevant to normal society. He writes within his experience of growing up in Indonesia and from his current life within the Church of the Servant King, an intentional church community in Eugene, Oregon. Appealing to biblical support for his claim, Sumantri asserts that discipleship is a matter of nationality, and that the very confession "Jesus is Lord" prevents an adherent of this confession from expressing political allegiance through voting.

---

1. Degan, "Electing Not to Vote," 61.
2. Whitmore, "When the Lesser Evil," 77.
3. Alexander, "Voting with Our Lives," 87.

Finally, I (Ted Lewis) close with an emphasis, similar to Sumantri's, on the ways that a political identity defined by voting is at odds with a political identity newly defined within a church community. Jesus's conversation with Pilate provides a template for a theological discussion of the way participation in the means of God (bearing witness to truth, loving others) best allows us to leave all outcomes in the hands of God. Jesus's "kingdom" language slides into "Caesardom" and "presidentialdom" language to stress the broader application of Jesus's view of the kingdom of God.

One limitation of all these essays is that they generally focus on American presidential elections and do not create specific dialogue around the ethics of state- and local-level voting. And what about referenda? Moreover, with the exception of Andy Alexis-Baker's essay, this book offers little discussion of decision-making models, whether of decision-making on micro- or macrolevels. Our hope is that additional writings will come on the heels of this volume to address the numerous other questions that remain.

Nevertheless, the aim of this book is to promote new thinking, new questions, and new dialogue where such thinking, questioning, and dialogue have not yet happened. Such dialogue will involve counterpoint and challenge, all to the end of helping people to act on firmer convictions and on principled reasoning. As all contributors have indicated, in addition to helping readers develop conviction for action, the aim of this book is to let the wisdom of readers' own faith traditions inform the shape of their political activity.

Ted Lewis
Eugene, Oregon
2008

1

Polls Apart: Why Believers
Might Conscientiously Abstain from Voting*

John D. Roth

In the late summer of 2004, I was visiting a Mennonite congregation in the Midwest where I had been asked to give several presentations. It so happened that the Democratic National Convention had just concluded the week before—disputes about the nature of John Kerry's military service were swirling in the electronic and print media, and the general nastiness of the campaign was becoming increasingly evident in op-ed columns, TV ads, and e-mail spam. As I walked toward the church, I noticed a small circle of men had gathered in the parking lot around two cars and were clearly engaged in a heated discussion. On the bumper of one of the cars a sticker was posted that read "George Bush *is* the weapon of mass destruction." The other car had a somewhat smaller sticker that read "W in 2004" against the background of an American flag. The five or six people participating in the debate did not look as if they were going to suddenly start hitting each other, but there was no mistaking the intensity of the exchange. As I walked slowly past the group, the fragments of conversation that emerged reflected the depth of the disagreement: "I can't believe you actually think . . . !"; "I'm so tired of your Bush bashing"; "It's a *stupid* war"; "At least he doesn't support baby killers!"

The conversation I overheard in the parking lot that Sunday morning was unusual only in the sense that it occurred in such a public place

* John D. Roth is Professor of History at Goshen College in Indiana, where he also serves as Director of the Mennonite Historical Library and as Editor of the *Mennonite Quarterly Review*.

This essay was originally published in Nathan Yoder and Carol A. Scheppard, editors. *Exiles in the Empire: Believers Church Perspectives on Politics* (Kitchener, ON: Pandora, 2006) 243–51. It is reprinted here by permission of the author and the publishers.

and so early in the day. In the fall of 2004, Americans throughout the country found themselves deeply divided in the midst of a nasty and divisive presidential campaign. To be sure, sloganeering, half-truths, and simplified versions of reality have always been a part of the electoral process. Yet most analysts have agreed that the 2004 campaign reached a new low—at least in modern memory—in terms of the personal vilification, mudslinging, negative campaigning, and outright fabrications on both sides of the race.

The caricatures were deeply entrenched. Kerry supporters attacked Bush as an ignorant, belligerent cowboy—a religious zealot who could only think about the world in terms of good and evil; us and them; patriots and terrorists. Bush supporters in turn branded Kerry as an elitist snob who waffled on key issues and was fundamentally unpatriotic. Add to this the familiar antagonism around such issues as the war in Iraq, tax breaks for the wealthy, gay rights, abortion, or gun control, and the split between the uncompromising extremes began to look like Grand Canyon. As the election wound to a close, it sometimes seemed as if we were living in two parallel universes with each side determined to reinforce its position by associating only with like-minded people.

Not surprisingly, the chasm dividing our country—along with the simmering tensions evident in offhand comments, eye-catching billboards, or partisan bumper stickers—became increasingly visible in our congregations as well. For the past two years I had been traveling widely in the Mennonite church, visiting dozens of congregations, staying in homes, talking with young people, and engaging in conversations with all kinds of people on topics related to "the gospel of peace" (Eph 6:15). The impressions I gleaned during that period—which happened to coincide with the long presidential campaign—are admittedly anecdotal; but in most of the congregations, I found people keenly aware of national politics and deeply interested in making a link between their Christian convictions and the outcome of the elections. At the same time, however, the nature of the conversation in most Mennonite churches seemed to reflect the tone and substance of the political discourse that was dividing the nation as a whole.

Now the fact of diversity within the Anabaptist family of churches regarding political engagement is not a new thing. The sixteenth-century Anabaptists were far from unified in regard to their understanding of the sword or how Christians should relate to government; and those in the believers church tradition have held a wide variety of positions on voting, political activism, and office holding. There is no well-established believers church "orthodoxy" on these questions. Indeed, it should be clear from the outset that the argument I wish to make regarding conscientious abstention from voting should not be understood as a standard of Christian integrity or faithfulness to Anabaptist principles. To be sure, our general commitment to pacifism and the voluntary church have always raised questions about the limits of our allegiance to the state; nonetheless, our traditions have also been characterized by a spectrum of political attitudes, ranging from vigorous engagement to a strict separatism.

What seemed new in the fall of 2004, however, was not the mere fact of diverse political attitudes but rather the growing "fundamentalism" evident among both the Christian Left and the Christian Right within our congregations, along with the sense that political involvement has now become a Christian imperative. I think we would all agree that the issues facing our country—issues of poverty and health care, housing, care for children and the unborn, security, relations with other countries—are all *moral* issues about which Christians might have something distinctive to say. But as I traveled in various Mennonite congregations, it became increasingly clear that the nature of the conversation about values and moral choices has been almost completely co-opted by the polarized rhetoric of the media: radio talk-show hosts, direct-mail campaigns, polemical ads, and Web-site bloggers. In short, our congregations do not seem to be ready or able to engage the substantive questions of this presidential election in a framework other than that of the Red/Blue divide in our national culture.

Although my invitation to "conscientiously abstain" from voting goes deeper than the divisive climate of the 2004 presidential campaign, this troubling reality forms an important context for my arguments against the civic ritual of voting. I wish to suggest five reasons that Christians might conscientiously abstain from voting. Even if readers do not find any of these arguments compelling, I hope that reflecting on them might encourage more deliberate discernment about the assumptions that we bring to bear in electoral politics in our dual role as citizens and committed Christians.

1. Not voting in the presidential election might be understood as a practical expression of our pacifist convictions. Those in the believers church tradition agree that the decision to become a Christian involves a choice, one with genuine consequences for our most basic understanding of reality. The heart of that choice is an affirmation of Jesus Christ as the one who saves us from our bondage to self-centered (or nation-centered) pride, and who offers in his life and teachings a model of the true nature of power—a power, as the Apostle Paul writes, "made perfect in weakness (2 Cor 12:9). "Becoming a follower of Christ implies more than just a "quantitative" change in our actions (where we become a little more moral, decent, or honest than everyone else); rather, it assumes that we will engage the world in a "qualitatively" different way. Indeed, every aspect of our lives should point to Christ's new understanding of power, expressed most dramatically in love for our enemies.

As commander in chief of the armed forces, the U.S. president is explicitly charged with the duty of maintaining the military, defending our borders, and preserving national interests through the use of violence if necessary or expedient. If I, as a follower of Christ, could not conscientiously serve in that role, then how can I in good conscience cast my support for someone else to do that in my stead?

2. From the perspective of an Anabaptist Christian, differences among the presidential candidates are illusory. George Bush frequently appeals to the notion of compassion (a good thing, in my mind), but is also a staunch defender of capital punishment (something I think Christian pacifists should not support). John Kerry seems to care about the environment (so do I), but his party clearly defends abortion (again, something I think Christian pacifists cannot support). Adding to the confusion, both candidates supported the decision to go to war in Iraq, both are committed to a "war on terrorism" that includes a very large role for the U.S. military, and both have assured the public that they are committed to some version of an "America First" perspective on the world. So which candidate is the obvious choice for pacifist Christians? We might recall that it was Jimmy Carter—the last overtly evangelical Christian in the Oval Office—who reinstated registration for the draft as a gesture of our military preparedness in response to the Soviet invasion of Afghanistan. In recent years, Mennonites and Brethren have voted overwhelmingly in favor of the Republican candidacies of Reagan and Bush. Yet I wonder whether these administrations—or that of Bill Clinton—really represent the deepest values of our faith. Rather than making a dubious calculation about the lesser of two evils in this regard, perhaps we should consider refraining from supporting either option.

3. *The "Constantinian logic" of voting our faith.* Nearly every Christian I have talked with about the subject of voting—whether inclined toward the Moral Majority on the right or the Sojourner alternative on the left—has insisted that there is (or should be) a connection between one's faith as a Christian and the outcome of one's vote. How we vote is an extension of our religious convictions. We vote on the basis of these convictions because we are convinced that society would be better if people who shared our convictions were running the show. Although we might feel a bit uncomfortable about stating it so bluntly, what we really mean is that people who believe as we do—Christians of our ilk—should be the ones holding political power and making decisions on behalf of the rest of society. The Moral Majority model of "reclaiming America for Christ," block by block, precinct by precinct, city by city may strike many as distasteful in its swagger, but the basic logic is actually one shared by Christians on the left as well—just with a very different political content.

Yet Christians in the believers church tradition should be very cautious about the "Constantinian logic" embedded in these assumptions. Having frequently been on the receiving end of theocratic governments throughout our history, we Anabaptist Christians might find it odd to be thinking now in terms of wielding the machinery of political power in order to advance our particular religiously informed causes, no matter how benign, enlightened, or morally "correct" those causes may be (something that Christians on both sides of the aisle assume is true of their position).

Our tradition has served the body politic best not as magistrates but in a prophetic role—questioning, challenging, discomfiting, and tweaking those holding power, reminding them that they are ultimately accountable to God for their actions. In 2003 Mennonites in the city of Goshen gained control of the city council. Four of the seven council seats are now held by Mennonites, while the mayor (a Goshen College graduate), is a member of the Church of the Brethren. Presumably, if the Mennonite city council members "vote their faith"—as Christian voters should do—their majority voice will soon be aligning our fair city more closely with the kingdom of God. Yet this prospect, not surprisingly, has evoked a great deal of grumbling and consternation in a city where Mennonites compose only about 20 percent of the population.

"No, no," Mennonites in the area have assured their worried neighbors: "Just because we are Mennonites doesn't imply that we think alike on the issues." In fact, one council member echoed the argument offered by John F. Kennedy in the controversial presidential election of 1960, with assuring words to the effect of "I'm a Mennonite on Sunday, but during the week I'm a citizen of Goshen. In other words, my faith is a personal and private matter. You don't need to worry that I will be dragging it into our city council debates or that it will determine the outcome of my vote."[1]

The insistence that local residents need not worry about a Mennonite theocracy—that faith convictions somehow turn personal or universal once the candidate is in office—brings me to a fourth argument for your consideration.

4. *The individualism and privacy of voting is in sharp tension with our communal understanding of faith.* If we actually do believe that we should "vote our conscience"—if responsible voting entails a process of moral discernment that is rooted in Christian convictions—then Mennonites and those in the believers church tradition should "be of one mind" about the matter and agree to cast our vote collectively. Most Christians, of course, would react allergically to the prospect of congregations' collectively deciding whom their members should vote for. Dragging politics into the church is unseemly; and, in fact, congregations could even lose tax-exempt status with the IRS if they did so! But if our faith is to have a bearing on the outcome of our choice, then shouldn't we agree on the candidate who best embodies our understanding of God's transformative work in the world, and cast our votes together?

On the other hand, if we are going to defend the privacy of the voting booth and the inviolability of individual choice, then we seem to

1. A more consistent Anabaptist position might have been for Mennonites in the area to consciously decide *not* to seek out the fourth seat on the council so as to remain in a minority role.

imply that our political choices are really of no great significance—more a matter of personal inclination or taste (some people like white bread; some like brown bread) than a profound expression of our faith. If voting is so important, then why shouldn't the church's voice in this important moral decision be more foundational to our choice than the political demagogues who currently dominate the radio and TV airwaves?

5. Not voting in national elections may have a symbolic and pedagogical value. In the past, members of the believers church tradition have paid a very high price for their "upside-down" view of power—loss of property, forced emigration, imprisonment, and even martyrdom have all been a part of our collective story. Now living in the lap of material abundance and prosperity, North American Mennonites could choose not to vote as a kind of "spiritual discipline"—a tangible reminder that our ultimate identity is not contingent upon the political process or dependent on the powers that be. Combined with a clear commitment to care for the sick, to feed the hungry, and to bind up the wounds of the hurting, conscientious abstention from the presidential elections could be a powerful symbol of our conviction that true power—the primary locus of God's hand in history—resides ultimately in the gathered church, not among the policy makers in Washington DC.

Voting, after all, is not just a "right." It is also a "rite"—a ritual of identity and loyalty binding the individual to the nation. Abstaining from presidential elections could signal to our children and to the global church that our first loyalty is to the worldwide fellowship of Christian believers, not to the nation-state.

Finally, there is a very personal dimension to my own decision to abstain from voting—an argument that will likely not be equally compelling to everyone. I happen to be passionately interested in politics: I read the papers regularly, follow the debates, and closely track the progress of each presidential campaign. As a twelve-year-old in 1972, I supported George McGovern's campaign against Richard Nixon with a deep passion; and I was crushed by Nixon's landslide victory that year when it seemed so obvious to me that he was misguided about Vietnam, callous toward the poor, and outright unethical in his campaign practices. I recognize in myself a strong temptation to become deeply enmeshed in the world of politics—to the point where I could easily believe that the most important force for change in the world really does reside in Washington or Ottawa or Tokyo or London, rather than in the gathered church where "Jesus is Lord." So for me, voting is a kind of spiritual discipline: a conscious restraint on my natural impulse to give electoral politics more attention than it truly deserves.

Some readers will undoubtedly regard these arguments for a "conscientious abstention" from voting to be ethically naïve, if not arrogant. Abstaining from voting, people often argue, does not make one any less culpable or responsible for political decisions of those in power. If anything, it makes one more accountable for these decisions because one did not speak out in support or opposition to those who are acting on behalf of the general society. All of us—voters and nonvoters alike—are implicated in a thousand different ways in the political structures of our country. To pretend that we can somehow "disengage" or claim some high ground of moral purity by not voting is disingenuous at best and outright irresponsible at worst.

In response to these concerns, I begin with a point of agreement: namely, that there is no place of "moral purity" for the pacifist Christian—we are indeed inextricably woven into the fabric of our communities; we are indeed implicated in the shadow sides of power and affluence. Because of this, I believe passionately that the gospel of peace calls us into the world—not to flee from it. My case against voting is *not* an argument for turning our back on the world's brokenness. Far from it! Christians—and especially Christians in the believers church tradition—should devote their lives to the healing work of reconciliation in their families and congregations, in their communities and countries, and in the world.

God loves this world—and we should be actively, creatively, passionately going about the work of extending God's compassion to all those around us. Christians should care about the *polis*. But at the same time they should not allow narrow definitions of "political involvement" to set the terms for how they should express that care.

Being "political" as a Christian can take many, many forms beyond active participation in a presidential campaign that culminates in a vote. The scope of these activities is extremely broad: you might choose to get involved, for example, in your local neighborhood association; or encourage your congregation to support homeless families through the Interfaith Hospitality Network; or volunteer for Habitat for Humanity. Consider giving a portion of your life in service to Brethren Volunteer

Service or Mennonite Central Committee (MCC); becoming a foster parent; adopting a child; becoming a surrogate grandparent to a child in a dysfunctional family; testifying before a legislative committee out of your experience "on the ground" with MCC; or speaking to your congressperson about what you have seen in your mission trip to Central America or your Christian Peacemaker Teams experience in Hebron. All these, and countless other forms of witness, are expressions of "political" responsibility. But Christians should be doing all this not as Democrats or Republicans but as a citizens of the kingdom of God; as a conscious ambassadors of Christ's incarnate body in this broken world; as followers of the Prince of Peace who rules "not by might, nor by power but by the spirit of the living God" (cf. Zech 4:6).

In the end, I do not wish to imply that my brothers and sisters in the church who go to the polling booths are being unfaithful Christians or are somehow turning their backs on the whole weight of the Anabaptist tradition. I readily acknowledge that my convictions against voting are much stronger for presidential campaigns than for local elections on county commissioners, school boards, or tax levies. But during the election-year cycle, when the airwaves grow foggy with appeals to our pocketbooks and our allegiance—as passions mount, and partisan appeals become increasingly reckless and extreme—I urge us to enter cautiously into the arena of national politics, to withhold absolute judgment about God's will in regard to any particular candidate, and to give at least some passing consideration to an older tradition of conscientious abstention from this national ritual.

2

When There Is Nothing to Vote For: Liberalism, John Howard Yoder, and the Church

Andy Alexis-Baker

> The revolution will be drowned in the ballot boxes—which is not surprising, since they were made for that purpose
>
> —Jean-Paul Sartre[1]

In November 2000 fifteen Canadians hungry for democracy went into their polling booths, pureed their ballots in a blender, and ate them. "There are no people to vote for in this election, only people to vote against," explained Mike Hudema, one of the members of the Edible Ballot Society.[2] Poll watchers went berserk, yelling, "Call the police! They are eating their ballots!" Elections Canada was furious. They ensured that the hungry voters faced charges of "willfully altering, defacing or destroying a ballot"—a crime punishable by up to three years in jail and a five-thousand-dollar fine.[3] The prosecutor justified the charges saying that the integrity of the electoral process was at stake.

By consuming their ballots, the Edible Ballot Society unmasked the sacredness of voting in North America. This quintessential democratic ritual is so self-evident that any challenge to it invites accusations of irresponsibility, insanity, or criminality. For the believers, the act of voting in a national election has intrinsic value as a "duty" and "obligation." Yet as John Howard Yoder once argued, voting is at best the weakest form of political action, anti-Christian mythologies surround the ritual, and voting does not change the basic fact that some people still rule over oth-

1. Sartre, "Elections: A Trap for Fools."
2. "Group Has One Way to Stomach the Choices."
3. "Ballot Is No Snack."

ers.[4] This essay will extend Yoder's observations to unmask some of the mythology surrounding "the national ritual" and to suggest that certain Christian practices point toward a less tense and dogmatic attitude toward elections in nation-states.

State Mythology

Through schools, media, and countless fragmentary ways we learn a foundational narrative that situates elections: the state saves people from violence and tyranny. In the United States, grade-school students learn stories of revolution and territorial expansion from textbooks, classroom discussions, and "fun" films like the *School House Rocks* cartoon shorts. Students eventually acquire a theoretical framework for this story from classical political theorists like Hobbes, Rousseau, and Locke. Under natural conditions, the story goes, individuals compete with one another over scarce resources, creating a "war of all against all."[5] So in order to protect their property and lives, people formed a contract: they surrender their "right" to violence to a centralized institution.[6] Thus the state (Hobbes's "mortal God") saves people from themselves and simultaneously protects each individual's self-interest without promoting any common or highest good.

Within this soteriological framework, students learn about democracy and elections. With the American and French Revolutions, the story continues, people broke free from monarchical tyranny and created a fundamentally new form of government: democracy.[7] Democracy transfers

4. Yoder, "National Ritual," 29–30.

5. Sheldon Wolin observes that rulers inscribe this state of nature—in which persons have a right to take whatever actions they think necessary to preserve themselves—into the nation-state with the phrase "reason of state." In "reasons of state," the sovereign claims a right to circumvent laws and norms, and to commit extralegal acts of detention, killing or other acts. "Reason of state" also forms the moral basis for the idea of revolution. See Wolin, "Democracy and the Welfare State," 483–85. This notion of "original war" differs from Christian accounts of original sin in that "original war" makes violence natural rather than sinful. See Manent, *Intellectual History of Liberalism*, 24.

6. For a critique of the "state-as-savior" see Cavanaugh, *Theopolitical Imagination*. For a concise yet more fleshed-out introduction to political liberalism see Manent, *Intellectual History of Liberalism*.

7. Stout, *Democracy and Tradition*, 203. Stout, however, claims that this classicist view distorts the slow evolutionary process that leads up to the modern democracies. However, Sheldon Wolin provides a powerful counterstory to Stout's in claiming that

the divine right of kings to "the people" and focuses elections as the ritual by which people exercise their divine sovereignty. In elections, individuals renew the social contract and consent to state rule so long as it helps save them from a common evil—starvation and death in the "natural condition." In elections, competing individuals once again agree to be social on the condition that their "rights" and interests remain protected.[8] Thus, in this mythology, individuals enact their "freedom" to be self-interested through elections; they do not deliberate upon a common good.[9]

Schools reinforce this story with student-government elections that form physical and mental habits in youth to automatically accept the underlying "state-as-savior" mythology. Studies show that the more educated a person becomes, the more likely they are to participate in elections and to have a high view of the system.[10] This mythology, supported by patriotic symbols and folklore, remains the dominant though unstated way in which people evaluate candidates for office. People learn to act without changing their fundamental belief system. Some sociologists and psychologists suggest that Sunday schools also aid in this process when they teach children that God is a "king" who created "the state." Studies show that these children then transfer their notions of God and Jesus to the presidential office.[11] So even if the media expose a crime that the president committed (like Watergate or the Clinton sex scandal), American society and churches teach children to distinguish the office from the person, so that despite "individual failures," the role remains ordained

constitutional democracies seek to discourage the "turmoil" inherent in real Athenian democracy in the name of "order." See Wolin, "Democracy: Electoral and Athenian," 475–77.

8. For example, during the 1994 election campaign, the Republicans' "Contract with America" promised that if Americans "contracted" with them in the elections, they would pass various legislative measures. See Rosenbaum, "It's the Economy Again, as Democrats Attack the 'Contract With America.'"

9. For a more sophisticated look at social-contract evolution and a critique, see Grant, *English-Speaking Justice*.

10. For example, twice as many college students aged 18–24 vote as do students in the same age range who are not attending college. The National Association of Independent Colleges and Universities (NAICU), which represents thousands of private colleges and universities in America, also claims that "the mission of America's more than 3,000 colleges and universities is the education of our nation's next generation of leaders, and the shaping of civic involvement in all graduates, irrespective of their career choices." *Your Vote—Your Voice*, 2.

11. Moore, *Child's Political World*, 228–31.

and worthy of respect and allegiance, and voting remains a "near-divine civil mandate."[12]

Elections as a Confession of Faith

The mythology of "state-as-savior" and democratic control, however, do not line up with empirical historical research. Historians have shown that rather than saving people from violence, state-making first arose out of organizing to fight wars.[13] William Cavanaugh has used these historical studies to argue that the nation-state is not "the keeper of the common good," as social-contract theories presuppose. Instead the nation-state usurps group loyalties and fragments attempts at real community.[14] Early modern people were aware of this danger. For example, when princes increased taxes to pay for rising costs of wars, and attempted to impose uniform language, currency, and religion across wide swaths of territory, people did not accept this state making easily. From 1489 to 1553, heavy taxes fueled six major rebellions in England.[15] Swarms of French peasants engaged in hundreds of antitax rights during the 1620s and 1630s.[16] Not only outright revolt but also weapons of the weak—"sabotage, foot-dragging, concealment, [and] evasion"—created "one of the most rebellious decades in European history."[17] Throughout Europe this widespread popular resistance forced state makers to negotiate their rule. Citizenship rights such as voting, therefore, did not come as a natural result of peaceable social contracts but as a result of struggles against state power.[18] Moreover, these rights were not benign but were specifically designed by state makers to undermine struggles against state making and to fragment social groups into individuals with "rights."

12. Yoder, "National Ritual," 29.

13. For example, see Tilly, "War Making and State Making as Organized Crime"; Ertman, *Birth of the Leviathan*; and Strayer, *On the Medieval Origins of the Modern State*.

14. See Cavanaugh, "Killing for the Telephone Company." I am indebted to Cavanaugh for pointing me to the historical sources cited in this article.

15. Tilly, "Reflections on the History of European State-Making," 22.

16. Ibid.

17. Tilly, *Coercion, Capital, and European States*, 101.

18. Ibid., 102. I have borrowed the term "citizenship rights" from Giddens, *The Nation-State and Violence*, 200.

Telling history truthfully is important. In terms of democratic theory, this history reveals that both the "state-as-savior" mythology and the story about transferring sovereignty to "the people" are equally false. Citizenship rights only intended to take the edge off of elite state rulers but never intended to shift sovereignty away from them. As John Howard Yoder has written, "We are still governed by an elite, most of whose decisions are not submitted to the people for approval. . . . The consent of the governed, the built-in controls of constitutionality, checks and balances, and the bill of rights do not constitute the fact of government; they only mitigate it."[19]

If democracy really masks a shift from one elite rule to another, then national elections are not as crucial to "freedom" as advocates of liberal democracy preach, and may actually be adverse to democracy and freedom. For example, Benjamin Ginsberg collected data on black voter demonstrations and unlawful political actions from 1955 to 1977 in the United States. In the 1960s, black voter registration and other forms of political action—violence, marches, and civil disobedience—dramatically increased. During this time, Congress passed several legislative acts favorable to black communities. When demonstrations and disobedience campaigns decreased in the 1970s, voter registration remained high; however, the government ceased passing legislation favorable to blacks. This change in the national legislative agenda shows that the government does not really respond to minority-voter interests and that voting *per se* does little to gain reforms.[20]

During the Vietnam War, college students burned draft cards, rioted, demonstrated, staged sit-ins, and orchestrated boycotts and strikes. They did not, however, demand that Congress lower the voting age to include them. Nevertheless, senators and congressmen regularly stated that the United States needed to lower the voting age to eighteen in order to draw young people away from direct action and to assimilate them into the system. For example, in a hearing on lowering the voting age, Senator Jacob Javits stated:

19. Yoder, "Christian Case for Democracy," 158–59. Contract theorists, however, might rightly reply that they were never trying to write history but to imagine what a rights-based society should look like. John Rawls describes his own position this way in Rawls, *Theory of Justice*, 136–42. Such theorists as Rawls, however, wrongly believe that they can write as if people have no history.

20. See Ginsberg, *Consequences of Consent*, 107–9.

I am convinced that self-styled student leaders who urged such acts of civil disobedience would find themselves with little or no support if students were given a more meaningful role in the political process. In short, political activism of our college-age youth today—whether it be in demonstrations or working on behalf of candidates like Senator McCarthy—is all happening outside the existing political framework. Passage of this resolution before this Committee would give us the means, sort of the famous carrot and the stick, to channel this energy into our major political parties on all levels, national, state and local.[21]

These examples show that instead of being an effective tool for change, voting is more like a confession of faith in the system as savior. Yet this confession is not always explicit until some folks make known that they do not vote. In 2004 I attended a campaign event for Green Party candidate David Cobb at a Methodist Church in Manhattan.[22] Prior to Cobb's address, several speakers repeatedly informed the audience about voter disenfranchisement: why the current voting system does not work, why the electronic system will lead to fraud, and other issues. Basically they claimed that the system excludes certain questions and people from having a voice. Then Cobb passionately begged the audience to vote for him.

During the question-and-answer time, I said that in light of such rampant abuse, exclusion, and powerlessness in the system (as they had all just admitted), perhaps it would be better to direct people's energies into a massive nationwide boycott of the elections. Abstaining from elections in such conditions is more of a political action than voting in a useless system. David Cobb replied, "That is the worst idea I have ever heard. It is dangerous and stupid."[23] He could not imagine such a thing because he had faith in the process despite all evidence that nothing good could or would come out of it. When someone challenges the efficacy and wisdom of national elections, people's trust in the system—however modest and limited that trust may be—and the nature of voting as a confession of faith become apparent.

21. Quoted in ibid., 12.

22. David Cobb and a group of election experts gathered before an audience on July 22, 2004, at Washington Square Methodist Church in New York City.

23. Cobb was correct on one score: widespread nonvoting would be dangerous. One fictionalized account of what might happen when people refuse the illusion of the ballot box comes from Saramago, *Seeing*.

Thus far I have argued that historically false and anti-Christian mythologies saturate American elections. The national and state election rituals do not present a way to decide upon the common good so much as a way to stamp with approval the state-as-savior mythology. Therefore, I question whether any way exists within the modern nation-state to deliberate a common good, and whether nation-state politics can only be self-interested. If individualism runs amuck in America, maybe it is because liberal democracy has worked all too well. Indeed when society conceives of itself as individuals contracting for their own self-interest, no way exists even to account for a common good, let alone to deliberate about it. Individuals simply become consumers in an electoral shopping mall where the same homogenous goods are packaged under different logos; democracy then becomes not deliberation on the highest good but managed conflict of mad shoppers. Voting within this kind of system is simply a meaningless act. The way that social-contract theories justify democracy is not historically, philosophically, or theologically viable. I believe, however, that the widely influential Mennonite ethicist John Howard Yoder provides theological resources for Christians to model another conception of politics.

Yoder's Better Hope

The mythology of the state-as-savior is a sample of the kind of assumption underlying "Constantinianism" that Yoder criticized.[24] First, this mythology tempts Christians to locate the meaning of history in a broad universal history rather than in the church's particularity.[25] Christians then focus on building up the nation-state rather than on building up the church as a political community where God reigns. Second, the state-as-savior mythology is Constantinian because, in the words of its best modern expositor, John Rawls, it imposes a special realm called the "political" upon people who "cannot enter or leave it voluntarily."[26] The state

24. "Constantinianism" is an arrangement in which the church's attitude towards violence and money shifts away from the New Testament pattern of pacifism and suspicion of wealth towards a "responsible" ethic suitable to dominating and ruling people who do not confess Jesus as Lord.

25. "What God is really doing is being done primarily through the framework of society as a whole and not in the Christian community" (Yoder, "Christ, the Hope of the World," 198).

26. Rawls, *Collected Papers*, 482. Yoder says about Rawls and the social-contract

demands allegiance, manufactures, and imposes allegiance. In Yoder's words, social-contract liberalism "describe[s] the nature of the hypothetical political system in such a way that every participant in the process can be told that they have responsibility for it. This is never really the case through the exercise of the vote, since (except in the most simple town meeting or village referendum) the franchise does not deal with all the questions but only with the choice of oligarchies."[27]

Christians infected with Constantinianism tend to have more anxiety over elections and over voting for the right person. Effectiveness becomes the criteria for voting. For example, Constantinian Christians will not vote for the candidate who they think best exemplifies Jesus's ethics, because to do so might "waste" their vote. They calculate whether or not to vote their conscience based upon circumstances ("Do I live in a swing state?") not in order to communicate a Christian message but to maximize their vote's perceived effectiveness in putting "the right" candidate into office.[28] Yet if Christians would recognize the mythology surrounding the electoral process, then the illusion of control would vanish, and they could "be less tense about which side to take, for the criteria which guide us may be more varied."[29] In his article "The National Ritual," Yoder examines Luke 22, in which Jesus states that the nations "lord it over" one another and claim the label "benefactors" (v. 25). Yoder's close reading of this text points out that Jesus simply recognizes the fact of some people ruling over others, with no illusions that such situations would cease to exist. Instead "our decisions about whether to try to be lords in our turn, i.e., about whether to believe in 'popular sovereignty' as a divine mandate to us all, like Jesus's own decision to be not lord but servant, belong in the context of this realism about power."[30] This realism about power should give Christians a restrained outlook on elections and free them from ideas that voting is a "duty" that enacts "freedom." Yoder claims that

models: "The entire thought pattern which we recognize in various 'social contract' or 'original position' phrasings is a logical outworking of Constantinian assumptions" ("Christian Case for Democracy," 169). I should also note that Rawls's use of the term *political* is reduced to defining the function of choosing which specialized elite regime should rule; the term does nothing to challenge the rules of the game.

27. Yoder, "Christian Case for Democracy," 170.

28. Compare this view with Yoder's view in *Christian Witness to the State*.

29. Yoder, "National Ritual," 30.

30. Ibid.

if Christians participate in elections with "lowered expectations as to real control" they will not be too uptight about whether to vote for the right or the left. They might even vote for the side sure to lose, so that the winners have less temptation to arrogance, or "we might ask to be counted against the system by abstention or by a throwing-away vote, supporting a hopeless cause."[31] Thus, a close reading of the biblical texts leads to different standards than does the shrill demand to be "responsible" with such a sacred duty as voting.

Contemporary Constantinianism also leaves Christians open to a social-contract model of the church, in which individuals come together in self-interested needs for therapeutic spirituality without transforming those initial needs into practices compatible with Christian faith. For Yoder, this view of the church impoverishes the practices that lend credibility to our corporate witness.[32] This is a vicious cycle in which Christians, because of "the inadequacy of contemporary ecclesiastical organization," place their hopes and energies into transforming the structures of the wider society so that through those structures humans transform themselves from selfish sinners to peaceable neighbors.[33] Impoverished church practices lead to seeking hope elsewhere, which only further impoverishes the churches and leaves the world without a credible model to point toward.

The alternative, according to Yoder, is to place our energies and focus in the local body of Christ. He outlines five "practices" that reveal the church as a political body that rivals the nation-state.[34] The practice that he calls "the rule of Paul" (1 Cor 14) describes church members gathering together to deliberate matters that affect the entire community. In this "open meeting," each person listens and waits upon the Spirit to move them to speak. Anyone who then has something to say "can have the floor."[35] Christian commitment to nonviolence supposes that we do not weigh majority power against minority weakness but discuss the merits of an argument, and in the process, the Spirit might open the way for a fresh

31. Ibid.

32. Yoder, "Kingdom as Social Ethic," 93.

33. Yoder, *For the Nations*, 113–14.

34. These practices rival the nation-state not in function but in terms of ultimate loyalty. Yoder discusses these practices in numerous places. His fullest discussion is in *Body Politics*. See also "Hermeneutics of Peoplehood" and "Sacrament as Social Process."

35. Yoder, *Body Politics*, 61.

direction that neither side had thought of (or considered) before. This type of meeting does not need a professional class of politicians or clerics; it needs "only the moderating that keeps it orderly and the recording of the conclusions reached."[36] The body does not come to any decision until its members have reached common judgments. In this way Yoder asks us not to "vote" in order to solve church conflicts or to make decisions, because voting "may reach a decision more rapidly but without resolving the problem or convincing the overpowered minority, so that the conflict remains."[37] Christians must cultivate the patience of nonviolence in their decision-making. As Stanley Hauerwas recently wrote, "At the heart of Yoder's understanding of politics is time, an apocalyptic time that means that in a world that too often assumes we do not have time to be political, Christians refuse to be hurried."[38] This applies not just to long-term rejection of war and violence but also to the short-term processes by which we make decisions: we refuse to be hurried and to conform to the world's process.

Yoder insists that this model can operate even in colleges and church agencies "just as efficiently as 'corporate models.'"[39] This process of dialogical discernment has been a fruitful current in Christian history. First Corinthians 14 sets forth the basic order for the *ekklesia. Ekklesia*—the assembly of free citizens in the *polis* (city) for governing decisions—signifies the political nature of the gathering. This *ekklesia*, with its process, created space for Corinth's socially marginalized to speak and act in ways that official city and imperial structures would not allow. The church council in Jerusalem, narrated in Acts 15, reveals the process in action. Throughout history, the larger Christian body has sought to embody the rule of Paul through church synods and councils, through disputations in the Reformation era, through Puritan and Quaker models of church order, and today through the World Council of Churches. In addition, New

36. Ibid., 67.

37. Ibid., 70. As Sheldon Wolin has said, "Majority rule, democracy's power-principle, is fictitious: majorities are artifacts manufactured by money, organization, and the media." Wolin's statement applies just as much to church-based decisions as to state-making. See Wolin, *Politics and Vision*, 601.

38. Hauerwas, "Democratic Time," 540. I am indebted to Hauerwas' article for pointing me to Sheldon Wolin's writings.

39. Yoder, *Body Politics*, 70.

England town meetings secularized the Puritan process.[40] This process was built for local, smaller-scale processes like the *polis* (city) and is not well suited for the nation-state.[41]

The rule of Paul exists at the center of a dynamic tradition of baptism, of breaking bread together, of giving and receiving counsel, of binding and loosing, and of reciprocal recognition of the gifts each brings, "giving special honor to the less comely members."[42] In these practices, just as in the rule of Paul, the church embraces conflict, knowing that "to be human in the light of the gospel is to face conflict in redemptive dialogue."[43] This redemptive dialogue is a "hermeneutics of peoplehood," in which Christians use the open meeting process—where Christians listen to their traditions in the Scripture and prophesy fresh directions on that basis—to practice becoming a unified forgiving community. Embracing conflict, Christians eschew weighing vote against vote or punishing or destroying the other side, and instead seek ways to win the other party, even at the cost of self-emptying. This is exactly what social-contract liberalism seeks to avoid through elections. Instead of affirming each person's dignity isolated from others in which the individual's freedom always conflicts with the group, New Testament practice affirms each person's dignity in relationship to the community—the body. Precisely because each person participates in the decision-making procedures, it is by definition impossible for the individual's convictions to conflict with the group's unity. If the individual and the group conflict, then the group has not come to unity yet, and the procedure still goes on.[44] The rule of Paul includes differences rather than denying them. The state's recourse to violence is ultimately the state's failure to be democratic; it inadequately imitates the voluntary associations of the Anabaptists, Quakers, and Puritans.

---

40. For a summary of Puritan influence on New England direct democracy see Lindsay, *Modern Democratic State*, 117–21 and Lindsay, *Essentials of Democracy*, 11–18. Yoder draws from Lindsay in "Response of an Amateur Historian," 417.

41. So instead of accommodating to the nation-state, perhaps we should be arguing against it in favor of other political forms. For an example of a Christian philosopher who argues against the state on these grounds, see MacIntyre, *Dependent Rational Animals*, 129–46.

42. Yoder, *Body Politics*, 50.

43. Ibid., 13.

44. Therefore, by definition the church is a body that seeks unity and forgiveness of one another.

If we take this vision of the church seriously, then communication and nonviolence become the primary criteria (rather than "responsibility" and "duty" to take charge of the state) for Christians to participate in any secular decision-making process. Too often, Yoder claims, Christians vote in secular elections to "become politically powerful and to use that power in the interest of one's own goals." Such a strategy is "hardly reconcilable with that of the New Testament church."[45] In the New Testament church, minority voices are given an extraordinary weight so that the majority cannot simply tread over them. Christians can and must apply this to their decisions on whether to vote and if so, how. Only when the candidates give Christians a tolerable option, and only when Christians actually have something to say about an issue (and to have something to say, they must be living out an option) should Christians participate in an election. Otherwise, "abstention as a testimony against corrupt politicians who give the electors no tolerable options because no real issues are at stake, or because the Christian brotherhood does not see clearly what needs to be said, would in many cases be more responsible than casting a vote without conviction on information or for sentimental or selfish reasons."[46] In the current American climate, with the democratic social-contract ideology that undermines the church's practices of deliberation, and with the corruption of corporate interests, abstention should be the normal Christian stance rather than the exception.

Conclusion

George Bernanos once stated, "In order to be prepared to hope in what does not deceive, we must first lose hope in everything that deceives."[47] Elections within the nation-state deceive us into thinking that we control the world. The philosophical move to place responsibility on every single individual for the American government is dubious for its presumptions and false in its practice. Indeed in such a system, eating one's ballot—as the Edible Ballot Society recommends—could be more of a reasonable response than voting for a barely tolerable candidate. A better hope comes from the Christian tradition, which refuses such offerings.

45. Yoder, *Christian Witness to the State*, 27.
46. Ibid., 28.
47. Quoted in Ellul, *Reason for Being*, 47.

This better hope, as Yoder articulates it, affirms the dignity of each person not in their isolation from others but in their relationship to the body of Christ. Special concern for the weakest members forces a process of dialogue and listening, of hearing Jesus in Scripture, and hearing the Spirit in the voice of the gathered community. Rather than weighing vote against vote, and majority power against minority weakness, this process waits on the Spirit, recognizing that a decision would not simply be that one side loses all, or that both sides have to win and lose halfway. Instead the Spirit can speak afresh. A way that neither party could have foreseen may unfold because of the special commitment to hearing God speak in this gathered process. By analogy, the town hall meetings of Puritan New England become the secularized version of this process. This is a process suitable for the *polis*, the city, but ill-suited for nation-states and their ever-expanding territory and moral grip. After reading Yoder, I find it is even harder to see how Christians can, with integrity, participate in the nation-state's charade. I, for one, will abstain from such endeavors to work for a better hope.

3

Freedom of Voice:
Non-Voting and the Political Imagination

Nekeisha Alexis-Baker

As a black Mennonite woman who is a naturalized American citizen, I am aware that refusing to vote in any level of electoral politics may offend members of at least four groups. Given that I am a black person, my decision not to vote may upset some African Americans, whose struggle for liberation included getting the right to vote. Since I am a woman, my decision not to vote may insult other women who praise the suffragist movement. Given that I am a naturalized citizen, my refusing to vote rejects a right and responsibility given to me as a foreigner with citizenship, a right and responsibility that other immigrants strive to attain. To some members of these groups my abstention from the electoral process wastes an opportunity to make my voice heard. My refusing to vote may also be perceived as dishonoring, if not revictimizing, those who risked life and limb to secure their vote in the United States. Not voting even offends some Mennonites who, tired of being the "quiet in the land," have steadily increased their activism, from participating in elections to serving in government positions. For the marginalized voices in American society, the right to vote is a sacred privilege that one should neither take for granted nor willingly renounce. Although I identify with these groups and have wrestled with these challenges, I no longer accept that voting is an effective way for people to exercise their political voices. Furthermore, when people see voting as the primary way to communicate their desire for justice to those in government, we hinder our political imaginations to our continued detriment. Instead, refusing to vote can liberate Christians from the American myth of voting-as-voice, can free us to speak in new ways, and can liberate us from seeing the ballot box as the most effective way to promote God's *shalom* in the world.

The Myth of Voting-as-Voice

During the 2004 presidential election, Declare Yourself, a national non-partisan nonprofit organization launched a voter-registration campaign titled "Only You Can Silence Yourself." Television commercials depicted an actor with his mouth bolted shut and with a drill in his hand, and an actress wearing a metal muzzle to illustrate what happens when young adults do not vote. Print advertisements showed photos of pop singer Christina Aguilera with her lips sewn shut and rapper André 3000 with his bowtie in his mouth, a single tear trickling down their faces. The campaign's message was clear: those who refuse to vote forfeit a chance to affect society, and subject themselves to a torturous silence. This message is not unique to the Declare Yourself campaign or to the 2004 election. The Women's Voices—Women Vote project encourages unmarried women to vote because "their voices are not being heard in our democracy";[1] and Rock the Vote reminds young adults of their "responsibility to speak out and push the nation to focus on the issues that are truly important."[2] For these and other voter-registration initiatives, the best—if not the only—strategy for citizens to voice their concerns on everything from health care in the United States and AIDS in Africa to tuition interest rates and underemployment is to vote in national, state, and local elections.

From an early age Americans are socialized to equate voting with voice. The children's book *The Voice of the People, An American Democracy in Action* states, "By voting on Election Day, American citizens participate in their government. They help decide how their cities, states, and country will be run."[3] Another children's civics book makes the point more succinctly, saying, "The people exercise their control by voting in elections."[4] Schools also teach people to value voting. The 1971 New York State Education Department guide for first-grade teachers suggested that students vote for a kickball captain or class helper to illustrate electing the president.[5] Television personality Spencer Christian provides another example of long-term socialization toward voting. As a child, his exposure to white people's denial of the black vote taught him to see voting as "a

1. Women's Voices–Women Vote, "Mission Statement."
2. Rock the Vote. http://www.rockthevote.com/censorsship/cen_index.php.
3. Maestro, *Voice of the People*, 3.
4. Hamilton, *Voting in an Election*, 4.
5. Ginsberg, *Consequences of Consent*, 39.

sacred right."[6] When he was an eighth-grade student, his civics education and role in a mock debate increased his fascination with the electoral process. Finally, as a college student, he volunteered to work on a few political campaigns. These experiences, Christian says, shaped him to see the importance of voting. Children's books, civics education, student elections, the immigrant-naturalization process and voter-registration campaigns train citizens to see voting as the most appropriate way to voice our concerns to those in government.[7] Despite this persistent message, I question whether voting is the best form of political action.

Voting advocates often overlook a simple fact: there is no space on ballots for people to share thoughts on issues that concern them. Ballots do not contain room for voters to indicate why they have chosen a particular candidate or to identify agreeable policies.[8] A ballot only has room to affirm prepackaged candidates whose vague plans have been publicized via sound bites, by negative campaign ads, in speeches, and in televised debates.[9] This point about the nature of ballots seems trivial until one watches politicians decipher what voters did or did not say at the polls. Such was the case in the 2006 midterm elections, in which the Democrats regained control of the House and the Senate. The *New York Times* declared that the election results put "a proudly unyielding president on notice that the voters want change, especially on the war in Iraq."[10] Exit polls revealed that four out of ten voters described the war in Iraq as an "extremely important factor" in their decision. In addition, six out of ten voters disapproved of the war's direction, felt that the war had not improved America's national security, and desired full or partial withdrawal of the armed forces from Iraq.[11] Although President George W. Bush initially acknowledged voters' disapproval with the war and vowed

6. Christian and Biracree, *Electing Our Government*, introduction, n.p.

7. Ibid., 32, 38–41.

8. Even if ballots allowed citizens to vote on public policy, I suspect it would be more detrimental to allow the majority to decide whether the state should enact laws for bilingual education, civil rights, or affirmative action.

9. According to Hill, *Fixing Elections*, mass communication has revolutionized the way politics is conducted. Of the thirty-second spots that permeate political races, he writes, "in a two-choice system, where you're carving up the electorate in such a way as to attract the most uncommitted, uninformed, muddle-headed swing voters, politics no longer requires either discourse or substance" and instead only requires candidates to cultivate an image to which the public can favorably respond (155).

10. Toner, "Loud Message for Bush."

11. Zelney and Thee, "Exit Polls."

to review his plans for the region, he then ignored a bipartisan proposal to bring order to the region and increased the number of soldiers to the area in a questionable "troop surge."[12] and leans towards an increase of up to thirty thousand troops in 2007.[13] Most notably, however, the president has reinterpreted the voters' message, saying, "I thought the election said they want to see more bi-partisan cooperation."[14] Meanwhile the Democratic Party, whom voters hope will change the war's direction, has not yet offered a clear alternative policy. Their victory instead produced vague rhetoric for "change," plans to investigate the Bush administration's management of the war, one senator's revived attempt to reinstate a military draft, and support from at least two prominent Democrats for Bush's plans to increase troop levels. The 2006 election shows that citizens cannot direct the government's actions through elections—even when the voice of the people seems clear.[15] Politicians choose how they respond to an election's results and, most important, retain the power to interpret what voters said in the first place.

Another flaw in the myth of voting-as-voice is that the polling booth is not always a reliable communication tool. The late-nineteenth-century "eight-box system," in which people voted by placing their ballots into several boxes, was especially susceptible to manipulation by white registrars, who moved the boxes to confuse black voters and invalidate their ballots.[16] Although voting technology has vastly improved since then, deliberate and unplanned disenfranchisement continues. In the 2000 presidential election, some New Yorkers were subjected to forty-year-old machines and a short supply of mechanics, while Floridians tackled optical scanners that voided legitimate votes, and to absentee ballots that were never counted.[17] One highly contested voting method in 2000 was the butterfly ballot, a confusing punch-card system with candidates' names

12. Rutenberg, "War Critics See New Resistance." See also Baker, et al., *Iraq Study Group Report*, 50.

13. Galloway, "Bush Is Still Not Ready to Listen to Dissenters."

14. Ibid. President Bush continued reinterpreting the 2006 election results in a White House press conference saying, "Americans are sick of the partisanship and name-calling. I will do my part to elevate the tone." Quoted in *The Hotline*, December 20, 2006.

15. Schier, *You Call This an Election?* 20–22. Schier argues that since political powers determine the important issues (agenda control) and people often vote against a candidate they dislike rather than for a candidate they favor (strategic voting), "Elections tell us remarkably little about the public will" (22).

16. Keyssar, "Right to Vote and Election 2000," 89.

17. Ibid.

on either side, which caused some people to vote for the wrong person.[18] As Harvard professor Alexander Keyssar notes, "Throughout the nation, and especially in poorer neighborhoods, votes were counted by ancient machines with extraordinarily high error rates. . . . Relatively few polling places had technology that would alert voters to mismarked ballots and permit them to vote again; in some where the technology was present, officials turned the option off."[19] The problems at the polls resulted in ballot recounts, court hearings, and eventually a Supreme Court ruling in George Bush's favor—even though Al Gore won the popular vote.

Like the election before it, the 2004 presidential race had its share of mechanical trouble. In Ohio, the Election Association Commission (EAC) provided $90 million to allocate machines throughout the state, yet the payment did not prevent "a wide discrepancy between the availability of voting machines in more minority, Democratic and urban areas as compared to more Republican, suburban and exurban areas."[20] Approximately four thousand votes were uncounted in one county alone due to anomalies in punch-card voting. Six years after Washington's $14 billion investment in new voting technology, problems continued as "tens of thousands of voters . . . encountered serious problems at the polls" in the 2006 midterm election.[21] Machine malfunctions led to over sixty thousand uncounted votes in Florida, and twenty thousand people were unable to vote in Colorado.[22] As director of Electionline.org Doug Chapin notes, "If the success of an election is to be measured according to whether each voter's voice is heard, then we would have to conclude that this past election was not entirely a success."[23] News of a lab's negligence in testing most U.S. voting machines cast even more doubt on past election results.[24]

Not only have voters been disenfranchised by mechanical error; people of color have been especially marginalized in the electoral process. Although the Fifteenth Amendment to the U.S. Constitution initially al-

18. Schier, *You Call This an Election?* 14.

19. Keyssar, "Right to Vote and Election 2000," 90.

20. House Judiciary Committee, "Preserving Democracy," 24.

21. Urbina and Drew, "Experts Concerned."

22. Ibid. Two national hotlines also received approximately 40,000 phone calls either about voting difficulties or requesting information.

23. Quoted in ibid.

24. Drew, "U.S. Bars Lab."

lowed blacks to vote and increased their political activity, politicians such as President Andrew Johnson, who vetoed bills to improve blacks' social standing and refused to challenge discriminatory laws in the south, hampered their overall progress. [25] Black people had lost most of their political gains by the early twentieth century.[26] In the 1890s southern states developed poll taxes, literacy tests, property requirements, and "grandfather clauses" to prevent black people from voting.[27] During the civil-rights era, whites suppressed Black votes through malicious and violent means. For example, their white landlord evicted activist Fannie Lou Hamer and her husband after Hamer's first attempt to register to vote. Night riders later harassed them by firing guns into their home. After registering on her second attempt, Hamer began organizing others to register.[28] After Hamer was arrested with other women following a voter-registration conference, her jailers allowed two male prisoners to beat her using "a wide piece of leather weighted with rock or lead."[29] Like Hamer, thousands of blacks who registered to vote were physically and verbally abused and were denied employment, financial credit, insurance, medical care, and access to stores.[30]

Individual acts of intimidation, deception, and systemic racism continue to thwart black votes into the present. Testimony during legal hearings by the National Association for the Advancement of Colored People (NAACP) on November 11, 2000, indicated that along with committing other human-rights violations, police harassed people of color who were on their way to vote; names of black people were purged from voter lists; legal requests for new ballots to replace spoiled ones were denied; and nonoperational voting machines were allocated to a historically black college.[31] The absence of bilingual ballots and language assistance at some of the polls also inhibited Haitian and Hispanic voters from casting ballots.[32] Other pernicious tactics to prevent people of color from voting resurfaced in the 2004 elections. Unknown persons in Ohio made calls

25. Zinn, *People's History*, 194.

26. Piven and Cloward, *Poor People's Movements*, 185.

27. Ibid., 187. See also Zinn, *People's History*, 285.

28. Norman, "Shining in the Dark," 173.

29. Ibid., 176.

30. Walters, *Freedom Is Not Enough*, 8.

31. Ibid, 98–99.

32. Ibid., 98. See also Keyssar, "Right to Vote and Election 2000."

to threaten potential voters and provide false information about polling locations.[33] Flyers from the nonexistent "Milwaukee Black Voters League" warned people that parking tickets would disqualify them from voting, while flyers in Pittsburgh misinformed others that Democrats must vote the day after the election due to expected voter turnout. Both flyers were distributed in largely black neighborhoods.[34] These and other abuses have created a strong distrust for the electoral process in the black community. Even one woman who diligently votes out of respect for black people's historical struggle "was convinced that no matter how she voted it would not be fairly counted."[35]

Although these examples of voter suppression undermine the myth of voting-as-voice, one may argue that electoral reform—not individual refusals to vote—is what the system needs. However, the government's attempts to alleviate failures in the electoral process are mainly superficial. Politicians may implement new voter-registration laws, but doing so does not change the fact that the laws are written by, administered by, and ultimately serve the major political parties rather than voters.[36] The EAC can pay for new voting technology, but doing so does not challenge alliances between lobbyists in the voting-machine industry and the political parties they support.[37] If the U.S. government is to attempt serious electoral reform, it must consider its critics' challenges to redistricting practices, to mass communication that distorts citizens' grasp of the issues,[38] and to

33. House Judiciary Committee, "Preserving Democracy," 63–64.

34. Urbina, "Democrats Fear Disillusionment in Black Voters." Fourteen thousand Hispanic immigrants also received flyers threatening them with arrest if they attempted to vote.

35. Ibid.

36. Keyssar, "Right to Vote and Election 2000," 91. Keyssar briefly describes the history of voter-registration laws and shows that they have served "as the rules of engagement between two hefty adversaries, each seeking to maximize its own turnout and minimize outright cheating by the other party."

37. Smyth, "Voting Machine Controversy." Smyth describes a controversy involving Ken Blackwell, Republican secretary of state in Ohio, and Walden O'Dell, former head of the voting-machine maker, Diebold Inc. O'Dell, who said he was "committed to helping Ohio deliver its electoral votes to the president," was set to receive a contract from Blackwell to supply voting machines for the 2004 election.

38. In *Fixing Elections*, Hill critiques these and other problems with elections, including the system itself. Of the fact that the candidate with the most votes wins and the loser gets nothing, he writes, "Worse than antiquated, Winner Take All [. . .] distorts national policy, robs voters of representation, and pits partisan voters, as well as racial, ethnic, and

the use of the electoral college instead of direct popular elections.[39] I do not expect politicians to pursue these and other extensive proposals for change at this time At this time when legislation on criminal penalties for those who deceive and intimidate potential voters cannot pass in the House or Senate.[40] Since "there is no groundswell for basic changes to the electoral structure,"[41] and since elections support the state's power, politicians have incentives to keep things as they are. Having little hope for radical electoral reform and a strong desire for freedom of voice, I choose not to vote. Yet if one abstains from voting, what, if any, options for political expression remain?

Political Imagination and the Body of Christ

As I encounter more Mennonites for whom voting is their primary or sole political action, I have concluded that some in my faith community are unable to think beyond the ballot box. Although I cannot speak for or about the entire Mennonite church, my relocation from a place with a wide range of political views to a largely Democratic Mennonite community has been an eye-opening experience. When I moved from New York City, I left behind a congregation and a subculture that were hotbeds of protest and came to a place where Sunday-school sessions, sermons, and prayers were preoccupied with the 2004 presidential election. Having left behind a community that respected my views on voting, I suddenly had to defend before fellow members of a historic peace church my refusal to elect the next commander-in-chief. Reflecting on this transition, I sense that some Mennonites are tempted to scratch a "Constantinian" itch, whereby they not only decide who runs the government but also seek to carve out a niche for themselves within the halls of power.[42] These people tend to see the government as truly political and to see the responsible

religious minorities against each other for [. . .] political representation" (xi).

39. Shier, *You Call This an Election?* 103–7.

40. See congressman Rush Holt's letter to the editor in *The New York Times*, November 3, 2006.

41. Schier, *You Call This an Election?* 139.

42. For Mennonite theologian John Howard Yoder, "Constantinianism" represents a recurring temptation of the church to shift attention away from building up its own life as a political community to building an alleged wider political kingdom in the world. See Yoder, *Royal Priesthood*, 198

Christian duty to be making history come out right in this system.[43] In this view, real political action is not singing hymns, preaching sermons, praying together, or sharing material resources; since God works "primarily through the framework of society as a whole and not in the Christian community," politics is writing letters to senators, volunteering for a candidate's campaign, serving on the city council, or voting in elections.[44] What follows, therefore, is that the life and practices of the congregation, though spiritually and emotionally uplifting, are not essential to or a sign of social change. Yet too often when Christians view government as the instrument for justice, they overlook the political resources of their own congregations. When they see voting as the primary way to influence the state's power, they risk limiting their political actions to ones that sustain rather than resist the status quo.

In *The Consequences of Consent: Elections, Citizen Control and Popular Acquiescence*, Benjamin Ginsberg argues that voting diminishes people's ability to participate in or support activities outside the electoral process. Citing studies from 1965 and 1972, he suggests that frequent voters are less attracted to disorderly forms of political engagement. In contrast, "individuals who, for one reason or another, have not been integrated into the electorate under normal circumstances simply do not participate, are much more likely to press their demands in a disruptive or even violent manner" and to support unruly forms of protest.[45] Far from being an avenue for social change or a way to use one's political voice, "elections facilitate participation [in government] in much the same way that floodgates can be said to facilitate the flow of water [. . .] diverting it from courses that may be hazardous to the established political order."[46] As a result, people who are committed to the electoral process, whether out of obligation or because it has provided tangible benefits, are less likely to participate in actions that threaten their personal security or the well-being of the ruling powers or society at large. On the other hand, whether they are officially excluded, whether they are disillusioned, or whether they conscientiously object to voting, those who remain outside

43. Ibid., 187.

44. Ibid. 198.

45. Ginsberg, *Consequences of Consent*, 58–59. For example, a 1972 survey conducted by University of Michigan found that people who reported "little or no past electoral activity" were more sympathetic to disruptive political actions than those who frequently participated in elections (56).

46. Ibid., 52.

the electoral process are more open to addressing their concerns in spontaneous, creative, and risky ways.

The civil rights movement is one example of a community that, denied access to regular political channels, resisted injustice and made their grievances heard in imaginative ways. Sit-ins, boycotts, and other forms of nonviolent civil disobedience highlighted black people's suffering in ways that white America could no longer overlook. Riots, looting, and armed self-defense revealed the extent of black rage boiling beneath the surface. One creative tactic that civil-rights activists used was freedom rides, in which blacks and whites rode on integrated buses to protest segregated accommodations in bus and train terminals.[47] When a group of freedom riders were attacked with clubs by a mob that grew to one thousand people, President John F. Kennedy had little choice but to support the group of riders, assigning four hundred U.S. marshals to protect them.[48] Within months, pressure from the rides compelled the federal courts and the Interstate Commerce Commission to desegregate all transportation terminals in the south.[49] Protesters also engaged in multiple forms of direct action over a sustained period of time. Such was the case in 1961 when the Southern Christian Leadership Conference (SCLC) helped organize lunch-counter sit-ins, plus marches, and boycotts of targeted businesses in Birmingham, Alabama. During the conflict, police unleashed dogs, fire hoses, and nightsticks onto thousands of unarmed people. As police brutality increased, several youth responded by rioting in the streets. A little over a month after the campaign began, the governor reached an agreement with the SCLC that desegregated lunch counters, rest rooms, and drinking fountains; that instituted fairer employment practices; and that released demonstrators from jail. The impact of the protests was far reaching, as President Kennedy pushed Congress to adopt a new civil-rights bill in June of 1963.[50]

Bolstering these forms of resistance was the black church. As C. Eric Lincoln and Lawrence H. Mamiya observe, "Black churches were

47. Ibid., 229. See also Zinn, *People's History*, 444–45.

48. Prior to the rides, Kennedy completely ignored letters for protection and ordered his civil-rights advisor, "Tell them to call it off!" Despite the begrudged protection, the FBI continually attempted to undermine the Freedom Rides by accusing them of Communist connections. See Kenneth O'Reilly, "The FBI and the Civil Rights Movement," 214–17.

49. Piven, *Poor People's Movements*, 230.

50. Zinn, *People's History*, 241–44.

the major points of mobilization for mass meetings and demonstrations, and black church members fed and housed civil rights workers . . . Black church culture also permeated the movement from oratory to music, from the rituals and symbols of protest to the ethic of nonviolence."[51] Black churches also served as fundraising and information centers.[52] During a boycott to desegregate lunch counters in Savannah, Georgia, worship at First African Baptist Church included boycott updates, offerings to raise financial support, and sermons encouraging members to join the campaign. Sunday afternoons were spent hosting rallies that packed the church.[53] For the congregations that took part in the struggle, these activities were not appendages to their life together. They naturally extended from the history of the black church as "a multifaceted, religious, social, economic, educational, cultural and *political* institution."[54] Described as "a nation within a nation," the black church provided black men with leadership opportunities that white society denied them.[55] The church was a place where black people, excluded from the polls, could vote for their church officials.[56] Black churches established their own literature and publishing houses, and their own institutions of higher education.[57] Most important, the black church shaped people's identity, so that one's pastor, church, office in the church, or denomination was integral to a person's self-understanding.[58]

In this highly communal context, worship, song, theology, and prayers could not be divorced from black Christians' protest. They "chanted and sang; they shouted and prayed; they collapsed in the aisles [of the church] and sweltered in an eighty-five degree heat."[59] Confronted by police and barricades, they knelt to pray and kept marching.[60] In mass

51. Lincoln and Mamiya, *Black Church in the African-American Experience*, 211–12.

52. Pinn, *Black Church in the Post-Civil Rights Era*, 14.

53. Billingsley, *Mighty Like a River*, 56.

54. Ibid., 9. Emphasis mine.

55. Frazier, *Negro Church in America*, 49.

56. Ibid., 48–49. See also Lincoln and Mamiya, *Black Church in the African-American Experience*, 205–6. Regrettably, black women were not afforded the same official leadership positions as men, and this sexism has persisted throughout the church's history. Thankfully, womanist theologians have risen to challenge this inequality.

57. Lincoln, *Black Church Since Frazier*, 113.

58. Ibid., 116.

59. Zinn, *People's History*, 443.

60. Young, *Easy Burden*, 222.

meetings they spoke of being delivered like Daniel from the lions' den; like Jonah from the whale; and like Shadrach, Meshach, and Abednego from the fiery furnace.[61] They sang hymns and spirituals—freedom songs that "were not a political or economic gift to the people from the authorities . . . [but a] gift of the people to themselves, a bottomless reservoir of spiritual power."[62] Ministers who spoke without fear of economic reprisal led and inspired the people.[63] The black church's rituals did not detract from political affairs happening outside their church walls; they were integral to the people's struggle for liberation. By the movement's end, the black church discovered "that it had a *power*, a potency it never before suspected."[64] Even when their voices were marginalized by whites and ignored by the state, black people could still shake society's foundation.

NonVoting and the Political Imagination

The civil rights movement illustrates effective ways for citizens to express their concerns or to voice their frustrations. As Ginsberg notes, "Spontaneous or privately organized forms of political activity, or even the threat of their occurrence, can also induce those in power to heed their subject's wishes."[65] More important than the effectiveness of the civil rights movement is the way it enabled black people to speak against their subjugation on their own time and in their own way. Unlike elections, with their firm schedule for political action, black people's "revolt was always minutes away, in a timing mechanism which no one had set, but which might go off with some unpredictable set of events."[66] Unlike voting, which excludes some people from participating, the movement included

61. Ibid., 231.

62. Ibid., 183.

63. Ibid., 209. According to Young, "No educated Black person was less vulnerable to pressure from the white establishment than a black Baptist minister." Because they received all their financial support from their churches and their congregations were entirely independent of white leadership and economic control, black clergy of all denominations were free to speak out against injustice in ways others in the community could not. As a result, they were essential leaders and motivators of the civil rights struggle. See also Lincoln and Mamiya, *The Church in the African American Experience*, 207. See also Lincoln and Mamiya, *Black Church in the African-American Experience*, 207.

64. Lincoln, *Black Church since Frazier*, 115.

65. Ginsberg, *Consequences of Consent*, 62.

66. Zinn, *People's History*, 442.

all who were committed to its goals. Too young to vote but old enough to understand that they suffered injustice, black children marched and protested segregation.[67] In one demonstration alone, hundreds of youth ages six to sixteen were arrested and jailed.[68] Describing their actions in Birmingham, Martin Luther King Jr. wrote, "A nonviolent army has a magnificent universal quality [. . .] some of the most valued foot soldiers were youngsters . . . the lame and the halt and the crippled could and did join up."[69] Unlike elections, which overemphasize individual leaders, the civil rights movement depended on the bodies of ordinary people like Rosa Parks, and on loosely organized groups like the Student Nonviolent Coordinating Committee (SNCC) to instigate and sustain it. An "institutionalized and routinized form of mass political involvement," voting cannot replicate the creative and inclusive potential of citizen-driven political actions; voting can even make these activities seem undesirable.[70]

1. Although voter-registration drives were part of the civil rights movement, activists did not unanimously agree on pursuing it. For example, while some members of the Student Nonviolent Coordinating, the Southern Christian Leadership Conference, and the Congress for Racial Equality welcomed the Kennedy administration's support for voter registration, others saw the administration's focus on voter registration as an attempt to "cool the militancy of the student movement and divert the youngsters to slower safer activity."[71] The issue was so contentious for the SNCC that it created separate divisions to tackle each strategy, in order to prevent a schism. Nevertheless, voter registration was a form of defiance within the civil rights struggle precisely because black people were being denied access to the polls. As such, activists like Ella Baker advocated both direct action and voter registration strategies. Although popular discussions of the movement limit its success to obtaining voting rights, activists like King did not prize the ballot at the expense of other freedoms.[72] Furthermore, non-

67. Ibid., 446.

68. Piven and Cloward, *Poor People's Movements,*

69. King, *Why We Can't Wait*, 38.

70. Ginsberg, *Consequences of Consent*, 6.

71. Zinn, *SNCC*, 59. See also Piven and Cloward, *Poor People's Movements*, 233.

72. Piven and Cloward, *Poor People's Movements*, 233. When the attorney general proposed that activists focus on voter rights, King said, "We would agree with the impor-

voting also won concessions. Piven and Cloward argue that "the rise of Black defections" during the 1956 elections helped force the signing of the Civil Rights Act of the following year.[73] Although activists worked tirelessly to register black voters, evidence suggests that voting did not improve blacks' social standing. Between 1955 and 1977, acts of civil disobedience decreased, and the number of black registered voters and elected officials increased. In this period, legislation favorable to blacks also decreased, and economic positions of black people deteriorated.[74] Given this situation, government concessions during the civil rights era "should be seen primarily as responses to violent or disorderly modes of political action on the part of blacks—sit-ins, demonstrations and riots—rather than as effects of black participation at the polls."[75]

Voting does not allow citizens to use their voices to elicit social change. Instead, freedom of voice and the potential to affect society are found when people broaden their definition of politics, when they see resources for action within themselves and their communities, and when they engage in creative forms of witness and resistance. Christians find freedom of voice when we realize that God's movement in history centers in the church. Within our hands we hold not the defective buttons of a voting machine but the possibility of a power that does not lord over one another. Finding our voices means losing our faith in the political option presented by a state whose primary goal is self-preservation. Nonvoting may be the first step to unlocking our political imaginations and to speak for justice with new voices.

---

tance of voting rights, but would patiently seek to explain that Negroes did not want to neglect all other rights while one was selected for concentrated attention."

73. Ibid., 215–17. The Democratic Party had not only lost the election because blacks voted for Republican candidates, but also because blacks stayed away from the polls. Black voter turnout declined in several Democratic strongholds, with a 28.5 percent drop-off in Boston, a 19 percent decline in Atlantic City, a 14.7 percent drop in Philadelphia, and a 12 percent decline in Chicago—all this in spite of the black population's growth in these and other cities. Piven and Cloward argue that this sharp and unexpected change in blacks' voting patterns forced Democrats to support the Civil Rights Act of 1957.

74. Ginsberg, *Consequences of Consent*, 106–7.

75. Ibid., 107.

4

Serving by Abstaining: Karl Barth
on Political Engagement and Disengagement

G. Scott Becker

To write a chapter on biblical reasons for not voting cuts against my grain. As it is, I find a troubling tendency among many of my fellow evangelicals to remove their theology from the political arena, as if responsible social action and participation in the well-being of one's city and country were not properly considered matters of Christian discipleship. I cannot advocate such a strategy, for our confession that Jesus Christ is Lord of all requires us to express that lordship over the intricate interconnection of social, cultural and economic conditions that form the stuff of secular politics. On the other hand, even more troubling is the large number of these same evangelicals who have entered forcefully and vocally into the political fray with a view toward imposing an ostensibly Christian morality upon a divided American public. If participation in the power struggles of governmental politics cannot but betray the cruciform character of Jesus's ministry, we must ask whether the church's mission can be harmonized with any exercise of political power, voting included.

My understanding of the church's role in politics reflects the blend of Reformed and Anabaptist traditions that form my Baptist identity. My Reformed inheritance teaches me to affirm Christ's lordship over the political sphere and to trust the Holy Spirit to move in that sphere to bring it toward relative conformity to standards of divine justice. As the progeny of Anabaptists, I see the conflict between the politics of the world and those of the reign of God, and I look to the visible community of disciples to embody a new political vision. For this reason, I look to Karl Barth for lessons on the relationship of the Christian community to the politics of the world. Barth stood firmly in the Reformed confidence that the world and its political processes belonged to God and were guided by divine providence. At the same time, as John Howard Yoder has argued, the arc of Barth's political thought drew him over the years into an increasing affinity with free-church ecclesiology.[1] A comparison of two moments in Barth's career, his formulation of a christological concept of the state as part of his resistance to Hitler, and his apparent political neutrality later in the face of the Cold War might shed some light on the question of Christian participation in the American electoral process.

Christ and the State

Barth left his native Switzerland to teach theology at Bonn at the same time that Nazi ideology began to emerge on the national stage. Although he at first considered the movement's ideas and leaders too absurd to sway the German public, he soon discovered that the church had not cultivated the theological resources necessary to resist its allure. When a German Christian Movement arose to bring the church into line with the Nazi agenda, a Pastors' Emergency League, including Barth and several other professors and ministers, gathered together to resist the state's encroachment upon ecclesial affairs. Meeting together at Barmen in May 1934, they produced their celebrated Barmen Declaration, in which they drew the lines that the state could not cross and announced their refusal to grant the *Führer* authority in the church.

However, while the Barmen Declaration is often and rightly praised for its courageous stand on behalf of the church, it has also received criticism for failing to condemn the Nazi regime itself or to address Nazism's specific social policies. The prevailing view of church and state among German theologians in the 1930s provided little basis for an all-out protest against the government, as long it left the church alone. In this view, the two institutions occupied two separate realms and carried out two separate tasks. The state was established to employ the coercive methods of the world to prevent sin from destroying the social order, while the church's mandate to proclaim the Word of redemption called for noncoercive methods that the world could not understand. Therefore, neither state nor church was qualified to speak to the other as to how it carried out its divinely mandated function.

1. Yoder, *Karl Barth and the Problem of War*, 111–16.

Barth found this view insufficient to address the then-current European crisis. In his treatise *Church and State*, he pointed out that unless there were a positive connection between the ethics of the state and the gospel proclaimed by the church, Christians had no basis for claiming, as most Protestants did, that earthly rulers were accountable to Christ.[2] Instead, he proposed that the state belonged under the heading of Christology. In other words, God had ordained the state not only to curb evil in a fallen world, but to participate in the redemption of the world through Christ. To support this argument, Barth turned to the language of "rulers and authorities" used in the New Testament to describe governmental powers and the spiritual forces behind them. According to Romans 13:1–7, these powers are established by God. But as Barth points out, the God who ordains the powers and the God revealed in Christ are one and the same. All earthly power, therefore, derives entirely from Christ and ultimately flows back to him. Although the powers have rebelled against their Creator, rejecting their God-given function and seeking instead to set themselves up as ends in themselves, Christ has overcome their rebellion through his death and resurrection. They have now been brought back into subjection to Christ so that, willingly or not, they serve his redemptive purposes, which are made known through the church (Eph 1:20–23; 3:10; Col 1:16–20; 2:10, 15; 1 Pet 3:21–22). Therefore the church has something to say about how the state carries out its task and whether some forms of government are more acceptable to God than others.[3]

In this view, the state's primary responsibility is to guarantee the freedom necessary for the church's proclamation of the gospel. This mandate to protect the gospel's freedom, Barth contends, is the one criterion by which the laws of the state can be judged. And it is sufficient. It rules out both anarchy and totalitarianism, both of which make freedom impossible, and renders the state accountable to "the justice, wisdom and peace, equity and care for human welfare which are necessary" for a true political order.[4] Therefore, the state has a right to require obedience to its laws, but it cannot claim sovereignty over all of life, for such a claim infringes upon the freedom of the Word. The state cannot require its citizens to

2. Barth, *Church and State*, 2–8.

3. Ibid., 23–36.

4. Ibid., 83–84.

express allegiance to a particular worldview, philosophy, or moral vision. The state is to be honored and obeyed, but not loved. "When the State begins to claim 'love' it is in process of becoming a Church, the Church of a false God, and thus an unjust State. The just State requires, not love, but a simple, resolute, and responsible attitude on the part of its citizens."[5]

The church, for its part, is to pray for the state. Paul commanded the church to offer up prayers, petitions, and thanks "for kings and all who are in authority, so that we may lead a tranquil and quiet life in all godliness and dignity" (1 Tim 2:2). But this kind of prayer, Barth maintains, draws the church into the sphere of governmental politics. To pray for the state is to take on a priestly role in relation to it, to bear responsibility for it, to call it to its best and to admonish it when it fails in its duty. The church is not to resent or endure the political order as a necessary evil but to desire it as a power created in the image of the heavenly city and taken up by God's salvific purposes. Therefore, Christians have a duty to promote a just government, one that guarantees the freedom necessary for the open proclamation of the gospel, the kind of political order that Barth finds incompatible with Fascism. It is not to be expected that such a state will establish true justice, but the value of its relative justice is not to be overlooked:

> Not as heaven (not even as a miniature heaven) on earth! No, this 'true order' will only be able to arise upon this *earth* and within the *present age*, but this will take place *really and truly*, already upon this earth, and in this present age, in the world of sin and sinners. No eternal Solomon, free from temptation and without sin, but none the less a Solomon, an image of Him whose Kingdom will be a Kingdom of Peace without frontiers and without end. This is what the Church has to offer to the State when, on its side, it desires from the State nothing but freedom.[6]

Specifically, Barth sees here a New Testament mandate for Christian activity in the cause of a democratic form of government. If through prayer we assume a priestly responsibility for the state, then subjection to governing authorities can no longer be seen merely as passive obedience. Rather, the church is to work toward a political order built on the responsible actions of the citizenry. Barth goes so far as to suggest that

5. Ibid., 74–77.
6. Ibid., 84–85.

this mandate could justify armed resistance against a totalitarian regime for the sake of a more democratic government:

> Can serious prayer, in the long run, continue without the corre-
> sponding work? Can we ask God for something which we are not
> at the same moment determined and prepared to bring about, so
> far as it lies within the bounds of our possibility? Can we pray that
> the State shall preserve us, and that it may continue to do so as a
> just State, or that it will again become a just State, and not at the
> same time pledge ourselves personally, both in thought and action,
> in order that this may happen, . . . reckoning with the possibility of
> revolution, the possibility . . . that we may have to 'overthrow with
> God' those rulers who do not follow the lines laid down by Christ?
> Can we give the State that respect which it is due without making
> its business our own, with *all* the consequences that this implies?
> When I consider the deepest and most central content of the New
> Testament exhortation, I should say that we are justified, from the
> point of view of exegesis, in regarding the 'democratic conception
> of the State' as a justifiable expansion of the thought of the New
> Testament.[7]

We can draw at least two ramifications from the connection Barth draws between Christ and the state. The first is that Christology has something to teach us about politics. This point comes out especially in the fourth volume of his *Church Dogmatics*, where Christ's threefold office as Priest, King, and Prophet becomes the lens under which sinful patterns in human society are exposed. In his priestly office, for instance, the Son of God willingly humbles himself before the Father, descends into solidarity with fallen humanity, and becomes a servant. The downward movement of the Son of God distinguishes the divine character from false notions of deity patterned after human pride. It deconstructs the image of an otherworldly, supernatural, distant, and authoritarian deity and reveals instead that true majesty consists in servanthood: "God is not proud. In his high majesty He is humble. It is in this high humility that He speaks and acts as the God who reconciles the world to Himself."[8] Barth goes on to show that God's self-revelation in the humiliation of Christ constitutes

7. Ibid., 79–80.

8. Barth, *Church Dogmatics* (CD), vol. 4, *Doctrine of Reconciliation*, part 1, 159 Citations in this essay from *Church Dogmatics* vol. 4, parts 1 and 2 refer to the first English-language edition, published in 1956 and 1958. Citations from *Church Dogmatics*, vol. 4, part 3, refer to the paperback edition (New York: T & T Clark, 2004).

an attack against social patterns grounded in human pride and the will to dominate. The divine will to become human, to serve, to be judged and to become helpless reveals the fallacy behind the human propensity to move in the exact opposite direction: to endeavor to deify ourselves, to dominate weaker parties, to remove ourselves from accountability, and to guarantee our security against calamity or attack. Our individual and collective aspirations toward self-exaltation are exposed as the very acts that rob us of our true dignity as covenant partners of the God who comes down.[9]

In a similar fashion, Barth presents Christ's kingly office in a way that critiques social failure to treat human individuals with dignity. As King, Christ is the Son of Man exalted into partnership with God. This exaltation affects every individual, for prior to any recognition or affirmation on our part, all human flesh has been joined in familial solidarity with our Brother Jesus Christ. When Jesus died, he made complete the solidarity of God with humankind; when he rose from the grave, he brought every human being with him into a majestic new status at God's right hand.[10] The kingly exaltation of the Son of Man exposes the personal and political laziness wherein we fail to grasp our true dignity as women and men exalted into partnership with God. In particular, it lays bare our inhumanity: our blindness to the fundamental connection we share one with another, to the fact that there can be no true good for oneself considered apart from the good of the human fellowship that God has gathered together in Christ. Resistant to the community into which we've been exalted, we learn to define our interests in consumptive and individualistic terms that make genuine interpersonal fellowship impossible. We learn to harden ourselves against the concrete material deprivations suffered by many members of our communities. Therefore, if the church is to bear faithful witness to humanity's exaltation in Christ, it must take up a public ethic that affirms the solidarity of the human community, the interdependence of people's true interests, and the right of every individual to livable material conditions.[11]

In the third part of his discussion, Barth describes Christ's prophetic office in a way that rebukes our social tendency to evade the Word of God.

9. Barth, CD IV/1, 418–68.

10. Barth, CD IV/2, 264–304.

11. Barth, CD IV/2, 432–52.

As Prophet, the living and present Christ, in the power of his Holy Spirit, reveals God's reconciliation with humankind as a vivid historical reality. That is, the Holy Spirit progresses through the world and its historical processes to make evident the fact that sinful humanity has been forgiven and raised up into new life by a gracious God. Therefore, this present age is not only a time of waiting for the coming of the kingdom. It is saturated with divine promise and meaning, with the presence of the risen Christ in our midst: "We are contemporaries of Jesus Christ and direct witnesses of His action."[12] As the living Word who speaks into our midst, Christ launches an attack against darkness and exposes our resistance against the light. Our resistance takes the form of evasion, a general unwillingness to hear and respond to truth that comes from outside our own experience. As a result of this evasion, public moral discourse generally takes the form of restating opinions already held by the majority, and of relying on courses of action that have already been tried in the past. Barred from discussion is the possibility that something radically new could break into human history to transform our relationships and social practices. Yet this is precisely what we proclaim in Christ. Therefore, the prophetic Word summons the church into open engagement with the world's political processes, not to dominate the discussion (for that would belie Christ's character as servant) but to introduce new possibilities for reconciliation and economic justice.

And this leads to the second ramification of Barth's christological understanding of the state: if the state belongs to Christ and ultimately serves his redemptive purposes, and if those redemptive purposes reveal themselves in history, then one can expect to find the Holy Spirit present and active in the public political arena. For this reason, Barth could insist that the church's ultimate task—to summon all people to faith in Christ—included a penultimate task: to work in cooperation with states and other institutions to bring about conditions that, relatively and provisionally, speak truthfully of humanity's reconciliation to God. The Christian community, Barth maintained, is "the society in which it is given to men to know and practice their solidarity with the world"; its members "are made jointly responsible for [the world], for its future, for what is to become of it."[13]

12. Barth, CD IV/3.1, 362–63.
13. Barth, CD IV/3.2, 773–80.

Christians enter the public arena as people with a particular message to deliver but also in need of correction and wisdom from non-Christian voices in order to better grasp the meaning and application of that message. The claim that Jesus Christ is the one Word of God does not in any way attribute epistemological privilege to his believers, but as Barth says, "it looks away from non-Christian and Christian alike to the One who sovereignly confronts and precedes both as *the* Prophet."[14] Rather, the church is to engage with the insights and truth claims of other groups, because the created lights from which these insights are drawn ultimately have their source in the one true Light, Jesus Christ. The church brings into the discussion a particular narrative that cannot be discovered unless it is told by its believers: the story of how Christ reconciled the world to God. But the implications of that story will not be in conflict with the true insights drawn from others sources of knowledge, for the One to whom the gospel testifies is also the Light that shines through every created light. Therefore Christians can speak the Word in a spirit of servanthood, proclaiming its social and political ramifications, and knowing that the Word of Christ and the truest aspirations of creation and human institutions will not be at cross-purposes with each other. The church can and should seek to integrate words from inside and outside the church, so that on the one hand, the wisdom drawn from other lights can be brought into the service of the Word of reconciliation, and so that on the other hand, the Word's service to the whole world can become evident to those outside the church.[15]

The church carries out this task through the ministry of evangelical address. Evangelical address, Barth explains, refers to the church's appeal to the world to respond to the claims of the gospel in concrete, historically contextualized ways. It is the church's invitation to the world to participate in bringing about social changes that, in limited and provisional ways, correspond to the kingdom. In its evangelical address, Christians assume that the offer of the kingdom "is valid and effective" for everyone.[16] The divided character of human society does not diminish the universal inclusiveness of the gospel. The church speaks on the basis of its conviction that the Word of reconciliation applies to all people, and invites groups

14. Barth, CD IV/3.1, 86–91.

15. Ibid.,135–65.

16. Barth, CD IV/3.2, 852.

outside the church to recognize their common interest in the ramifications of that message:

> Evangelical address as the community's ministry of witness means the inclusion of all men near and far, from the very first and without fastidiousness even as the great sinners they are, like all members of the community. It means the bringing of all into the picture in the most literal sense. It means their incorporation into the likeness of the kingdom of God which is to be offered, into the circle of the validity of the content of the Gospel and therefore of grace, of the covenant, of reconciliation, of God's humiliation accomplished for the world in Jesus Christ in order that man might be exalted. In evangelical address the community, with a full awareness of what it is attempting, but constrained to make the attempt, strides across the frontier which separates non-Christian humanity from itself as the elect and calling people of God, taking the frontier seriously in the sense that, neither optimistically nor pessimistically but in faithfulness to its mission, it does not regard or address them as Jews or various kinds of heathen, as atheists, skeptics or indifferent, as victims of error, superstition or unbelief, nor as the total or partial hypocrites they may seem to be, but as the people of *christiani designati*, so that while the barrier between them is not destroyed it is removed in the act of encounter and common ground is occupied.[17]

"While the barrier between them is not destroyed it is removed in the act of encounter and common ground is occupied." For Barth, the claim that the divine decision for all humankind has been pronounced in Jesus's act of reconciliation means that the divine Word applies to every individual and to all social institutions, inside the church or outside. Because this Word relativizes every human word, Christian or non-Christian, it belies any notion that the church can dominate the public discussion or ignore its own dependence on wisdom from other sources. And because the Word is the Light that produces every other light, Christians can participate in discourse with a variety of groups and traditions, fully expecting to find resonance. The Spirit of Christ has gone ahead of us into the world's social dynamics to begin the transformative work of forgiveness and reconciliation in their midst. The church enters confidently into the arena of public politics because that arena belongs to Jesus Christ.

17. Ibid., 853.

Barth between East and West

In light of the political character of Barth's theology and his open resistance to National Socialism, many of his contemporaries were understandably puzzled by his apparent indifference toward the rise of Communism in the 1950s. As will be seen, however, Barth's unwillingness to commit to the Western cause does not reflect disinterest or ambivalence toward the political sphere. Rather it was a form of political protest shaped by specific social concerns and informed by careful theological analysis of then-current events. As such, it provides a resource for today's Christians as we consider the possibility of abstention as a form of political engagement.

In the days leading up to the Munich Agreement of 1938, Barth called upon his Czech friend Josef Hromádka to use whatever influence he had to mobilize a military resistance to the German army. He warned, "The freedom of Europe stands or falls with the freedom of your people," and he urged Czech citizens to use whatever means possible to defend their borders.[18] When the Korean War broke out in 1950, interpreted by many as evidence of the threat that communism posed to the world's stability, religious leaders throughout Western Europe turned to Barth, hoping to hear a similar call to action. His silence prompted church leaders to adapt his previous exhortation to their current situation. The pages of the theological journal *Christ und Welt* proclaimed: "Since Germany today is in the same situation vis-à-vis Stalin as Czechoslovakia was vis-à-vis Hitler 12 years ago, love of freedom must take precedence over the love of peace."[19]

This provoked Barth to declare the intent behind his neutrality and to make clear that the current situation differed sharply from that of 1938 in a number of important ways. First, to begin with, in 1938, Europe confronted a turning point, and Barth had seen that failure to discern the times could have consequences for generations to come: "The dice fell then. At that moment the East-West problem was unfurled. And at that moment Europe and Christendom slept. That was the time to cry out."[20] By contrast, Barth considered the so-called crisis of 1950 to be the out-

---

18. Karl Barth, letter to Josef L. Hromádka, September 19, 1938, in Barth, *Offene Briefe 1935–1942*, 113–15.

19. Quoted in Wolf-Dieter Zimmermann, letter to Karl Barth, October 13, 1950, in Barth, *Offene Briefe 1945–1968*, 203.

20. Karl Barth, letter to Wolf-Dieter Zimmermann, October 17, 1950, in ibid., 207.

working of the decision made twelve years earlier—history's judgment, so to speak, on Europe's earlier inattentiveness. The church's task at such a time is not to sanction the consensus of a nervous populace trying to ward off the consequence of its past, but to remind the people that God has not abandoned them to their fate and that they need not be afraid.[21]

Second, whereas 1938 witnessed a clear aggression of a powerful force against the stable social order of a free people, the situation in 1950 looked more like a confrontation of ideologies. In spite of the threat posed by the Soviet Union, Barth asserted, war was not inevitable, and the church had a duty to say so. The church was to expose "every natural lust for war, delight in war and warlike provocation" as the real enemy, and to warn against the destructive potential latent in the assumption that one ideology must conquer the other. The path to real security, he admonished, was not to destroy the opposing ideology but to listen to it and learn from it. The West, for instance, would do well to learn from Russia's critique of the economic disparities rampant in capitalist societies. Barth advised, "Whoever does not want Communism—and none of us wants it—will not set out against it at the gates, but will set out for a serious socialism! Today's sleepers are those who do not have this understanding. And to make it understandable is the Christian task today."[22]

Third, differences between the Czech and German national characters and situations made it impossible to apply one set of principles to both nations and at separate times. Where the Czechs had demonstrated an aversion to war throughout their recent history, Germans had shown themselves willing to send two consecutive generations of young people into battle for the sake of national self-aggrandizement. If the church had a duty in 1938 to awaken a people reluctant to fight, its task now was to exorcise a nation's volatile militarism. Generalizations concerning the limitations of pacifism or the threat faced by the free world were of no help here; only careful attention to each country's particular history could guide the church in its task.

Barth's refusal to come down on the side of East or West reflected not a withdrawal from the sphere of international politics but a deliberate protest against the rebellious claims put forward by both sides. Without denying the tyrannical character of Stalin's regime, Barth exposed the

21. Barth, letter to Zimmermann, October 17, 1950, in ibid., 207.
22. Ibid., 210.

temptation among Western powers to shield themselves against God's judgment and grace in relation to their own past, to assert the truthfulness of their ideology over another, to ignore the divine rebuke against economic injustice, and to nurse a long habit of domination through military violence. Barth recognized that he was being asked to enlist in the West's project of self-deification. In light of Christ's priestly humiliation, he could not lend his voice to the service of the hegemonic claims of one party or the other. Nor, with a view to the new human status revealed in Jesus's kingly exaltation, could he participate in Western efforts to evade the call to economic justice implicit in socialist doctrine. Finally, because Christ as Prophet was revealed in history, Barth understood the Christian mission to entail not only proclaiming the Word but also applying it to the concrete political concerns of the day. The church may have to carry out this task by refusing to endorse one party or another, but its neutrality is not benign. The church's neutrality is an open rebuke against the self-deifying claims and dehumanizing practices on both sides.

Conclusion: A Time Not to Vote?

This brief comparison of Karl Barth's political engagement and disengagement at two critical moments in history suggests a number of reasons for Christians to stay involved in the electoral process of a democratic country. In the first place, if we understand the New Testament to say that Christ has not only defeated the powers but also has brought them back into the service of God's redemptive purposes, then the church has something to say to government about how those purposes play out in public policy. In a democratic country, voting is one of the most readily available venues for delivering such a message. Second, as Barth points out, the command to pray for our leaders places us in a mediating role with the state, a role that implies responsible solidarity with the body politic. To the extent that the task of public decision-making belongs to the citizenry as a whole, to withdraw from the decision-making process is to break away from that solidarity. Third, as spelled out in the *Church Dogmatics*, the downward movement of the Son of God and the upward movement of the Human One expose the fallacy behind political structures that either reinforce hegemony or betray the dignity of the human individual. Democracy, at least in theory, is designed to break down hegemony and to empower the individual citizen. Through their participation, Christians testify that this form of government expresses the human situation in Christ more truthfully than many of the alternatives presented throughout Western history. Finally, if the Word of Christ declares itself in history, both inside and outside the church, then we have reason to expect to find the Holy Spirit at work in secular politics. The Spirit's presence there should be taken as a summons to the church to enter that arena.

Of course, the optimistic depiction of democracy implied in the previous paragraph is often belied by the way it actually works itself out. We can't trust a political system to bring about what can only be accomplished through repentance: the correction of deeply rooted tendencies toward self-deification, inhumanity, and evasion. More often than not, a constitution's loftiest ideals serve to mask rather than rectify a nation's collective sins. When the mutual ambition of both political parties to dominate and marginalize the other has eliminated the possibility of honest self-criticism or of multipartisan efforts toward the common good, or when all viable candidates have become so beholden to wealthy and powerful supporters that no one is left to speak for the voiceless—for those living in poverty or without health care; for those who, because of race, criminal record, or immigration status are deprived basic rights or legal guarantees; for creation; for those with developmental disabilities—a sudden, widespread Christian abstention from the electoral process could serve to expose the hypocrisy that has seeped into it. Most of all, when partisan political animosity has infiltrated the congregation so as to divide the body, or when the cause of Christ has become conflated with the limited agenda of one particular political party, then the time has come for the church to withdraw from political activity for a season in order to listen again to the voice of the One in whose name we speak. By extending our roots more deeply into our theological soil, we can prepare ourselves to present in truth and in unity the hope that gospel brings to existing social structures.

When Christians abstain from voting in order to expose the self-deification and inhumanity of the political process, or in order to examine their own distortion of the Word of God, their disengagement serves as a form of engagement. It is a testimony to a better way of doing politics and a rebuke against a system that has abandoned its high calling. As such, choosing not to vote should not be undertaken as a private matter of conscience but should be undertaken publicly and collectively as the church's witness to the world.

5

Electing Not to Vote: Whether Choosing Red or Blue, Politics Is Love of Mammon

Michael Degan

Shortly after the 2004 presidential election, I was sitting with two young women from my Mennonite congregation during our annual relief sale. During a break, we shared coffee and some donated homemade cookies. One of the women lamented, "How about that election? Is that depressing, or what?"

"Yeah, I'm thinking of moving to Canada," joked the other woman at our table.

Both were clearly displeased that George W. Bush was still president. They looked toward me, awaiting my commiseration.

"I didn't vote," I said, a bit sheepishly. They responded with blank, confused expressions and wondered how a committed Christian could sit out such an important election, with war and peace at stake, and such seething anger all around. How could I be so seemingly apathetic?

But I was not apathetic. In fact, I was just the opposite. I had decided not to vote in that election after a long and torturous inner struggle in which I sought to reconcile what I hoped to gain against what I seemed to be losing within myself. Was the vision of God's kingdom for which I was ostensibly working, hoping, praying—and voting—honored by participating in a political culture that seemed to bring out the worst in me; that led me to demonize those on the other side of my views; that caused me to think, feel, and sometimes act, in a word, unchristianly?

Not of This World

For a practicing Mennonite fifty or more years ago, to refrain from voting would not have seemed unusual. The Mennonite doctrine of nonconformity held that Christians should separate themselves from the world, and that separation included nonparticipation in government at all levels. Christians should not only refrain from voting but from holding political office. Adherence to biblical nonresistance also required that Christians avoid serving in the military or working in occupations that required coercion or the use of force, such as police officers or prison guards.

Much of this doctrine was once loosely described as "two-kingdom theology," a theology that systematized the dichotomy that Jesus described when he said that his kingdom was "not of this world" (John 18:36). Mennonites took Jesus's saying to mean that while the world was governed by the political and secular institutions under which people lived, the soul was governed by God's kingdom as revealed in Scripture, and therefore loyalty to the worldly kingdom was superseded by faithfulness to the heavenly one. Christians were to submit to those who governed them on earth, but that submission did not include sharing in the earthly power of those governments or legitimizing it through politics.

For Mennonites, two-kingdom theology was articulated by twentieth-century theologians like J. C. Wenger, who in the mid-1960s described a course of noninvolvement in politics:

> Surely the church needs more than ever to give its witness against every form of injustice, whether it be against the maltreatment of the poor by the rich or the maltreatment of minorities by the majority. It is in proper order for individual Christians, for congregations, and for conferences to speak out in favor of justice and against all unrighteousness.
>
> The central function of the church of Christ is not merely to try to abolish all forms of evil and injustice. The most basic function of the church is to proclaim the everlasting Gospel to the salvation of men and their gathering into the blessed fold of the redeemed. Our supreme guide here is the teaching and example of our Lord and His apostles. First-century Christianity was dynamic; it began an amazing transformation of human society—a transformation that turned the world right side up: but it did so not by political methods but by the faithful proclamation of the Word of God. [1]

Wenger was no doubt responding to the political activism that was growing during his era, when many Mennonites were slowly moving away

---

1. Wenger, "Nonresistant and Nonpolitical."

from the separation that he and others advocated. Like other Christians, many American Mennonites prayed, hoped, and worked for an end to the Vietnam War, racial segregation, and other types of injustice entering popular consciousness.

Two-kingdom theology has now been all but abandoned, and the thinking of many mainstream Mennonites is that Christian witness requires some participation in American political life. Consequently, many have taken sides in the "red/blue divide" and have fallen prey to its heated rhetoric and partisan inclinations.

Christians of all political and theological persuasions now tend to see their role as electing politicians who represent their values, and who will work to bring about their vision of God's kingdom through political activity. We expect these politicians, once they are in power, to craft laws, nominate judges, appropriate funding, pass resolutions, and generally promote the kind of world in which God will achieve some kind of victory over God's enemies, who are, more often than not, those who disagree with us.

I found myself breathing in this hostile atmosphere during the 2004 presidential campaign season. Indeed, to some extent, it had always been part of my political participation. But the stakes in that election somehow seemed higher. With the war in Iraq raging aimlessly, and the shock and awe of September 11, 2001, still relatively fresh in the American consciousness, the 2004 election seemed more momentous and weighty than any I could remember. At the same time, the political climate had turned more base, ignoble, and vile—yet more superficial—than ever before.

Was this sorry state of affairs something in which Christians should be taking part? How did this activity fit with Jesus's call to love neighbor as well as enemy? Had Jesus's great commission to "make disciples of all nations" been reduced to merely putting like-minded Christians in charge of everything?

It began to seem to me that perhaps the Mennonites of old, and today's conservative Mennonites, were on to something by rejecting involvement in politics and government, including voting. Did they perhaps recognize that political participation ultimately leads to a compromising of gospel values? Were they more willing to accept the consequences of leaving the ugly grab for power to others?

So an examination of some of that doctrine and two-kingdom theology may be apropos. It doesn't require a search for a lot of discarded books and documents, because many conservative, "plain," and Old Order Mennonites still adhere to much of this doctrine. They continue to publish tracts, pamphlets, and small books, while making sure that older volumes of theology and doctrine stay in print.

The Anabaptists in these traditions generally cite two reasons for avoiding politics and voting: the separation of the two kingdoms and the commitment to nonresistance.

Under the two-kingdom rationale, traditional Mennonites consider heaven as the kingdom to which they belong. The kingdom of the world, they would say, is the realm of Satan:

> Conservative Mennonites have a policy of noninvolvement in government and politics. They refrain from voting, holding political office, and serving on juries. They will not swear oaths or serve in any branch of the military. They may appeal for exemption from a law that they cannot obey, but they do it without any threat or other form of coercion to gain their end. Christians are citizens of the heavenly kingdom and are "strangers and pilgrims" in this world (1 Peter 2:11). [2]

To vote or to participate in government identifies one with "this world," not with Jesus's kingdom:

> God sets up the civil powers; they are "ordained of God" (Romans 13:1). He sets up and puts down rulers according to His sovereign will. . . . Voting in national, state or local elections would identify us with a kingdom of this world. It would associate us with civil powers in a program we could not be part of or carry out—such as the war machine, the police force, retaliating and bringing vengeance. . . . Would not the church member voter be trying to serve two masters? [3]

Voting brings with it repercussions and responsibilities to which Christians adhering to the path of biblical nonconformity and nonresistance cannot in good conscience subscribe:

> The exercise of the franchise [i.e., voting] according to the [U.S.] Constitution makes an individual an integral part of the government. My nonresistant conscience forbids me to hold an office in which I should have military authority, such as the governor

---

2. Null, *Introduction to Mennonite Doctrine and Practice*, 67.
3. Hartzler, *Christian and the State*, 6.

or president possess. Since I could not serve in any such capacity, I feel I have no responsibility to share in the election of such officers.[4]

In many communities, voting also places one in the jury pool. Jury duty is a civic obligation that Mennonites were once encouraged, in some cases required, to avoid. It necessitates the swearing of an oath—a violation of Mennonite doctrine, based on Matthew 5:33–37—and could, in a capital case, result in the death penalty, which would violate nonresistance.

Commitment to Nonresistance

Christians are to submit to their government, as Romans 13 commands, but they are not called to participate in it because they may be required to use violence to defend it. They are to trust the Lord for their well-being. Voting indicates a lack of trust in God's benevolence, as does seeking revenge, or worrying about "what you will eat or what you will drink" (Matt 6:25):

> [The Christian] supports his government by paying his taxes and by obeying laws fully, making exception only when he is asked to do something he believes to be contrary to God's law. The Christian does not make a practice of complaining about the existing government, but feels that the authorities are appointed by God for our protection. The Christian in defending the nonresistant position maintains that since he does not want to assume the obligation of carrying arms because it is contrary to Scripture, he ought to refrain from exercising the power of government by way of holding office or voting, but submit and obey the powers that be in every way that he can conscientiously.[5]

If we are fully committed to nonresistance as commanded by Scripture, then we must be willing to accept the consequences that may come from refusing to take up arms and from refusing to have a say in who directs the armed forces:

> [When we vote,] we become responsible for the actions of the government and the killing even though we refuse to fight. This we deny, maintaining, as God's people have done in the past, that we are not a part of the carnal government and want no part. Why

4. Lehman, "Christian and Civil Government," 44.

5. Horst, *Christian Nonresistant Way of Life*, 40.

then should we, by voting, acknowledge that which we so strenu-
ously deny by our refusal to fight or hold public office?[6]

A Christian who fully trusts in a loving God leaves the formation of
God's kingdom to God:

> A further argument in favor of voting is sometimes raised when
> moral issues are at stake. . . . The Christian can safely put this mat-
> ter in the hand of the Lord and pray, "Thy will be done." God can
> very easily look after any political repercussions we might fear. The
> Christian glorifies and serves God best by maintaining a strong,
> active faith in His sovereign power to manage all the affairs of the
> political world.[7]

This notion of trusting God for our well-being is a recurring theme
in traditional Mennonite theology, as this passage from *Doctrines of the
Bible*, first published in 1928, demonstrates:

> The idea that it is the duty of the Church to take hold of Government
> and run things for God is neither taught in Scripture nor sup-
> ported by the facts of history. The place for Christian people to
> take hold and work is in the Church. . . . When Christianity was
> adopted as the religion of State in Rome, the result was that Rome
> corrupted the Church instead of the Church purifying Rome. It is
> ever thus. . . . The idea that the Christian can render substantial aid
> in the cause of righteousness by "mixing in politics" has often been
> proved a delusion.[8]

Voting Christians for the most part believe that they make their country, state or town a better, more moral place by electing politicians with
values and beliefs similar to their own. But many traditional Mennonites
believe this a self-deception:

> Many well-meaning people feel it is their God-given duty to try
> to influence the government to do what is right. They think that a
> Christian should at least vote, so that the proper people are elected.
> . . . It is true that some men are guided by moral principles more
> than others, but we never know what a man will become when
> elected to public office.[9]

6. Horst, "Nonresistance and Nonparticipation in Civil Government."
7. Martin, *Christian and the World*, 79.
8. Kauffman, *Doctrines of the Bible*, 174.
9. Martin, *Christian and the World*, 78.

Despite all this doctrine, voting among Mennonites throughout American history has been relatively consistent with voting among the general population, according to *The Mennonite Encyclopedia*, published in 1959. "Only in recent times," its article on voting says, "have some more conservative individuals concluded that they should not vote because it presumably involved them in the support of men in offices which they themselves could not occupy." [10]

Cynicism toward the Process

Examination of some of this doctrine from the early twentieth century changed my thinking about participating in government and politics. I now view nonresistance as more than just not fighting back and turning the other cheek. It is commanded of us because it indicates complete and unconditional trust of God, as Jesus requires.

Participation in partisan politics had led me to compromise on the biblical principle of loving my enemies. My zeal for winning the election, the debate, or the argument made it impossible for me to respond with love to those on the other side. I was in fact a slave to hatred, which in twenty-first-century American political life is becoming a seminal value.

That hatred is no doubt fed by a growing cynicism with the political process. An honest look at how we elect our representatives reveals that the choice, such as it is, has less and less to do with the ordinary voter. Much of the choosing is done behind the scenes by political operatives who maneuver conditions over which voters have little control. The choice is really no choice at all.

One example of this lack of choice is in redistricting, the process by which congressional districts in each state are determined. Redistricting has become highly litigious and politicized, but it is vital in helping the majority party remain in power. It works like this: Every ten years when the census figures come in, whichever party is in power in a particular state is permitted to reconfigure that state's congressional districts according to the new population numbers, a process called "gerrymandering." Invariably, the majority party will rework district boundaries in such a way as to carve up the districts held by the minority party, thereby helping majority incumbents and hurting minority ones. The majority party often

10. Dyck and Martin, *Mennonite Encyclopedia*, 4: 860.

gains seats in following elections, strengthening its majority status while making districts less and less competitive.

But if the majority changes hands, voters in the new minority party can find themselves suddenly represented by the new majority party. Voters who may have been represented for decades by one party can have their district wiped out. They become part of a new district and are represented by someone who may know or care little about their needs and problems.

Redistricting is nearly always contentious, and without fail, the minority party shouts, "Unfair!" and files a lawsuit before the ink is even dry on the new district boundaries. The cases then usually drag through state courts for a year or two, during which time the public loses interest even as their voice in representative government is being silenced. The cases are frequently very complex, taking turns and touching on issues that few voters understand. Most greet the issue of gerrymandering with a big yawn.

Redistricting has had three disastrous impacts, according to the League of Women Voters. The first is a sharp decline in the number of competitive seats in Congress and in the state legislatures. After the last round of redistricting in 2002, only four incumbents in the House of Representatives were defeated by challengers—the smallest turnover in U.S. history. In California, not a single seat in Congress or in the state legislature changed party hands in the 2004 elections. This lock on power has led to a second consequence, an ideological polarization in American politics. And the third negative result has been that leaders of both parties, spurred on by this consolidation of their political muscle, have become all the more aggressive in gerrymandering the districts in their states.[11]

Other factors too illustrate the loss of real choice in electoral politics. These factors include the concentration of ownership of the mainstream press (both print and electronic) by a few large corporations, and the astronomical amounts of money needed to undertake and win a modern election. Both of these factors help to shape the tenor and content of debate, such as it is, in American elections.

11. Mann, "Redistricting Reform." *National Voter*, June 2005, 4–6. Accessed February 1, 2006. Online: http://www.lwv.org.

National versus Local Elections

Thus far much of what I've said about voting has been in the context of national elections, especially presidential politics. Most Americans react viscerally to issues that are often tied in an almost religious way to patriotism and nationalism. Candidates who have the power to make or prevent war often appeal to the deepest sense of morality within their supporters. Clever politicians know how to push buttons connected to notions of sacrifice, love of country, and duty in ways that cajole us into taking sides. We allow our political choices to become moral choices, even though they are, truth be told, self-serving in the end. We no longer see those on the other side as merely disagreeing with us over this or that issue. We see them as enemies who can have no good in them because they are not on our side. The stakes are high in national elections, and the politicians never let us forget it.

It is ironic, then, that national politics gets so much attention when it is really local and state governments that have a far greater and more immediate impact on the average voter. Yet local elections rarely evoke the strong emotions often seen in national politics. Exceptions to this trend occurred recently in the state where I live: Pennsylvania.

State legislators up for reelection here were quaking in their boots as November 2006 approached. The reason: a pay raise that the lawmakers quietly voted for themselves and for the state's judges in July 2005. The size of the raise varied, but the increases were as high as 54 percent for some offices. Though state law prevented the legislators from taking the raise in the middle of their terms, many collected the money as what they called "unvouchered expenses." For judges, however, the raise was effective immediately. In an unprecedented move, voters showed their anger by refusing to reelect a sitting state Supreme Court justice to a second ten-year term.[12]

Lawmakers heard the message loud and clear. Eight days after the election, they repealed the raise. A record number of challengers came forward to run in the spring primaries, and more than sixty incumbents found themselves facing opponents within their own parties.[13]

As voters statewide took out their anger over the pay raise on their local representatives, angry taxpayers in the Dover school district dis-

12. Associated Press, "Legislative Pay Raise before Pennsylvania Top Court."
13. Raffacle, "Sixty-one Incumbents Face Primary Challenge."

missed all but one member of the school board in a case that received much national and even international attention. Voter anger here centered on the school board's unanimous mandate that teachers of ninth-grade biology were to read a statement at the beginning of the semester casting doubt on the theory of evolution. The statement referred students to an intelligent-design science textbook, which was said to be available in the schools' libraries. Eleven parents sued the school board in federal court, claiming the policy was an effort to introduce creationism into the public schools and therefore violated the establishment clause of the U.S. Constitution. There was a six-week trial, and the judge in the case did not issue his ruling before the November 2005 election. Nonetheless, voters in the school district, fed up with the controversy and embarrassed by the policy, rejected eight of the nine school board members who were up for reelection.[14]

Both these cases show that voters hold more sway in state and local elections than they do in national ones. This seems natural, since voters are more affected by what happens in their towns and states than by what happens nationally, except in rare cases. This is not to say that voters are *unaffected* by national politics, just less affected than seems apparent from the media attention paid to national politics. The voter choice slowly but surely diminishing in national elections can still, for the time being, be quite potent in state and local elections.

But voters must work very hard to effect change at the local level, and as soon as they are not paying attention, hard-fought gains can be reversed. In Kansas, for instance, intelligent-design supporters on the state school board were in the majority in 1998, removed in 2002, but returned in 2004. According to *USA Today*, "Caroline McKnight, director of Kansas' non-partisan Mainstream Coalition, says that's because 'people took for granted that . . . we'd already fought this battle.' The lesson for both sides: 'You can't ever take for granted who's in that last slot on your ballot.'"[15]

Changes like kicking out an entire school board or energizing a "throw-the-bums-out" movement against incumbents succeed through careful organizing of an angry electorate. Following these issues closely

14. Lawrence, "'Intelligent Design' Backers Lose in Pennsylvania."
15. Ibid.

enough seemingly requires a preoccupation that borders on obsession. And that's clearly not what we are called to as Christians.

But aside from the more dynamic power of choice that voters may have in local elections as opposed to national ones, the hostility, anger and hatred that motivates those choices is just as prevalent. For me, this places voting at any level in the worldy realm, not the heavenly one.

Some might argue that the November 2006 national elections, in which the Democrats took control of the U.S. Congress, show that electoral politics "works," and that voters were able to force a change in leadership. Expectations are high for major changes, especially regarding the Iraq war.

But all that really has occurred is that the flip side of the coin has been granted control. The coin remains the same. And one senses a mood that voters are not so much entrusting Democrats with a sacred duty, but rather that voters are punishing the Republicans for poor results in Iraq.

God or Mammon?

I've cited some ways that the choice voters are supposed to have, at least on the federal level, is not really a choice at all. Some of these behind-the-scenes tactics that disenfranchise voters are less apparent on the state and local level. But another reality is in play. Despite any policy differences one could cite between the two major American political parties, the two parties are really more similar than they are distinct.

While it's true that Republicans and Democrats are polar opposites on some issues, neither party is really interested in reform or fundamental change. In fact, they work toward just the opposite. It is the nature of a political party to be concerned primarily—perhaps solely—with achieving and maintaining power. And though many American politicians trip over each other to brandish their Christian credentials, they have everything to lose from a true Christian ethos that denies the self, loves the enemy, and prefers the poor to the powerful.

The claims of some politicians notwithstanding, genuine Christian values of love, humility, and service are generally tossed aside when one steps into the political arena, whether to cast a vote or to receive it.

Democrat and Republican are two sides of the same coin—a coin that Jesus called "mammon." And this is the choice we must make. Not between Democrat and Republican but between the alternatives that Jesus offers: God and mammon. "No one can serve two masters," Jesus reminds us (Matt 6:24). We must choose.

I have come to recognize that when I vote, I am staking a claim to a piece of the mammon. And no matter what kind of world I think I'm voting for, when I engage in politics, I am ultimately working for what is in my own self interest. In order to vote, I must decide who my enemy is. And I must work for my enemy's defeat. How can I love my enemy when I do that? I have not found a way to vote and to love my enemy at once. Nor have I found a way to respond with love to my enemy's attacks and still stay in the contest. Political operatives use the language of hate toward opponents because it works. As a disciple of Jesus, I choose to speak that language no longer.

What does God really want from us in the end? Has God taken sides in the prominent political issues of our time? Is God rooting for us to make abortion illegal, to end the war, to wipe out poverty, to prevent gays from marrying? Does God need our political machinery to establish the heavenly kingdom on earth?

I have discerned that God does not operate that way. I believe that God is watching us most closely when we stand face-to-face with those who disagree, oppose, or resent us. How do we react? With love or with hate? In God's way or in the world's way?

I reject voting not because there is anything intrinsically wrong with it, but because of who I become in order to win. When I join in that contest, I can't help but succumb to the hatred.

Christians are called to proclaim the kingdom of God, not necessarily to create it. Creating is God's divine work. When we try to create the kingdom, we undertake a self-serving and vain exercise in which we choose friendship with the world, and by so doing choose "enmity with God" (Jas 4:4).

6

When the Lesser Evil Is Not Good Enough: The Catholic Case for Not Voting

Todd David Whitmore

On November 2, 2004, I stepped into the voting booth and made my selections for city, state, and congressional officials. However, for the first time since I started voting (1976: Carter versus Ford), for reasons of conscience I did not vote for a presidential candidate. I made my decision based on Catholic teaching. I have been teaching and writing about Catholic social teaching in the theology department at the University of Notre Dame for fifteen years and am director of the university's Program in Catholic Social Tradition. In gathering facts on any given policy case, I make sure to read both the *New York Times* and the *Wall Street Journal*. If the *Times* is, in words attributed to Alasdair MacIntyre, the newspaper of "self-satisfied liberals," then the *Wall Street Journal* is the read for self-satisfied fiscal, and sometimes social, conservatives. In other words, I make my decisions with an informed conscience on both theoretical and practical levels. I reflected long and hard about whether to vote in the presidential election. What follows is my thinking on the matter, and it moves in three parts: the general obligation to vote, the specific case for not voting, and the obligations that remain after not voting. I will set out my thinking in conversation with the United States Conference of Catholic Bishops' 2003 document, "Faithful Citizenship: A Catholic Call to Political Responsibility," which they wrote to help prepare Catholics for the 2004 elections.

I: The General Obligation to Vote

Catholic social teaching begins with the claim that persons are inherently social—meaning that they are inextricably interdependent and thus have positive obligations toward one another that extend well beyond the idea of tolerance. In the Catholic view, rights are not simply negative protections against incursion from other people; rather they are, in the words of the U.S. bishops, the "minimum conditions for life in community."[1] Even what are typically termed "negative" civil and political rights—like the right to vote—require positive action on the part of people to make them manifest. This was evident in the 2000 election, where poor voting mechanisms left "hanging chads" on voting cards and put the veracity of the presidential election in doubt.

Because it begins its social analysis with an understanding of persons as interdependent and carries with it the consequent view of rights as conditions for participation in community, Catholic social teaching does not discuss rights apart from duties. The fact of interdependence means that any right implies a corresponding duty. Catholic teaching discusses the obligation toward others under the general rubric of the duty of solidarity. In contrast, contractarian thought, which has become predominant in the United States, posits that people join (or contract into) political society simply to protect their *own* interests. Rights here are understood to be simply negative immunities from incursion on one's zone of autonomy, and tolerance—the noninterference with others—is the primary duty. Solidarity is a much more robust concept and practice than tolerance, as is evident from the following quotation from Pope John Paul II:

> It is above all a question of interdependence, sensed as a system determining relationships in the contemporary world, in its economic, cultural, political, and religious elements, and accepted as a moral category. When interdependence becomes recognized in this way, the correlative response as a moral and social attitude, as a "virtue," is solidarity. This then is not a feeling of vague compassion or shallow distress at the misfortunes of so many people, both near and far. On the contrary, it is a firm and persevering determination to commit oneself to the common good; that is to say the good of all and each individual, because we are all really responsible for all.[2]

1. National Conference of Catholic Bishops, *Economic Justice for All*, heading for chapter 2, section B2.

2. John Paul II, *Sollicitudo Rei Socialis*, par. 38. Unless otherwise indicated, all citations of Catholic social teaching are of the paragraph numbers. Also, unless otherwise indicated, all translations are from O'Brien and Shannon, *Catholic Social Thought*.

The right to vote follows from the duty, in solidarity, to the common good. Voting is one way in which Christians can exercise this solidarity. In *Gaudium et Spes*, the Second Vatican Council discusses the right and duty to vote precisely in terms of communal participation on behalf of the common good. It is "in full accord with human nature" to "participate freely and actively" in the political order. "Hence let all citizens be mindful of their right and duty to vote freely in the interest of advancing the common good."[3] The American Catholic bishops, in their 2003 "Faithful Citizenship: A Call to Political Responsibility," follow this line of reasoning as well: "In the Catholic tradition, responsible citizenship is a virtue; participation in the political process is a moral obligation. All believers are called to faithful citizenship, to become informed, active, and responsible participants in the political process."[4]

Although the American bishops recognize that faithful citizenship is "about more than elections," they never take up the issue of the limits of the duty to vote.[5] What is a "faithful citizen" to do if all the viable candidates in a particular election are not simply wrong on this or that policy but are so egregiously in error from a moral as well as a political standpoint that one cannot in good conscience vote for any of them? The bishops do not address this question, in my analysis, because in repeatedly using the term "faithful citizenship" without serious theological grounding, they conflate the object of Christians' primary citizenship—the city of God—with the human city.

The indiscriminate joining of the terms "faithful" and "citizen" makes it seem as if the conscientious decision not to vote is an act of bad faith. This is particularly the case because the bishops identify any refusal to participate in the political order as "retreat": "At this time, some Catholics may feel politically homeless, sensing that no political party and too few candidates share a consistent concern for human life and dignity. However, this is not a time for retreat or discouragement."[6] In Catholic teaching, few specific duties are absolute, including voting. The conscientious decision not to vote in a particular election is not a "retreat"; rather it is an act of solidarity on behalf of the common good. The American

3. Second Vatican Council, *Gaudium et Spes*, par. 75.
4. United States Conference of Catholic Bishops, "Faithful Citizenship," 5.
5. Ibid.
6. Ibid., 3.

bishops' conflation of the city of God and the human city makes it appear as if the duty to vote is absolute.

II. The Specific Case of Not Voting

Catholicism has a longstanding tradition of providing the grounds for opposing state or society. The ultimate ground for such action is the distinction between the city of God and the human city or, otherwise put, the eternal law and its reflection in the natural law on one hand, and human law on another. The two sides of each equation are not necessarily opposed, but neither do they always coincide. There are limits to the claims that society or the state have on us. The two prime cases exemplifying this fact are, in the economic order, the case of legitimate "theft" in instances of extreme need and, in the political order, the case of civil disobedience against unjust governmental action.[7] Not voting in a particular election is a much milder form of selective nonparticipation than either of these cases.

My analysis of George W. Bush and John Kerry finds that both fall far short of what Catholic teaching can affirm on both foreign and domestic issues. I must limit my analysis of each candidate to one foreign and one domestic matter. I examine President Bush's policy in the Iraq war and his tax policy; I investigate Senator Kerry's positions on the Iraq war and abortion.

George W. Bush

There are multiple moral problems with the U.S. involvement in Iraq. The issue goes beyond whether U.S. involvement violates this or that particular criterion of the just-war tradition as articulated by Catholic social teaching. There are so many moral problems with the engagement that one must look behind these problems to the theological substratum. In the early days of the engagement, Bush administration officials used the moniker, "Operation Ultimate Justice" and referred to U.S. action as a "crusade." Not until religious leaders protested did the administration

7. On legitimate theft in instance of extreme need, see Thomas Aquinas, *Summa Theologica* II-II, q. 66, a. 7; and Second Vatican Council, *Gaudium et Spes*, par. 69. On civil disobedience, see, for instance, John XXIII, *Pacem in Terris*, pars. 51 and 61.

back off of these terms.[8] Actions since the terminological change indicate that it was a shift in words only. The distortion of intelligence on weapons of mass destruction, the efforts to skirt the Geneva conventions with regard to the treatment of detainees, the overriding of the criterion of last resort in favor of a doctrine of "preventive war," and the largely unilateral action all indicate that the administration does in fact think that it is fighting on behalf of ultimate justice. In the Christian tradition and in other monotheistic traditions, however, only God's justice is ultimate. The claim of ultimate justice on the part of the administration is not simply a violation of this or that norm of the just-war tradition; it is a violation of the first commandment.

The most accurate read of the various violations of the specific just-war norms is in terms of this first (theological) violation. Entities that hold that they uniquely represent ultimate justice tend to breach moral norms. This is why Catholic leaders have never embraced the idea of "supreme emergency," where, as Michael Walzer writes, "we are under the rule of necessity, and necessity knows no rules."[9] To suspend the rules of warfare under threat from an attack, no matter how severe or imminent that threat might be, is to make one's own civilization into an ultimate good. It is, in a word, blasphemous.

Catholic leaders have stopped short of leveling the blasphemy charge, though Reverend Pasquale Borgomeo of the Vatican has referred to the "propagandistic attitude" of the Bush administration, and *Civilta Cattolica*, the Vatican newspaper, stated the concern that "in the depths of the soul of the United States, there is a sort of messianic vocation on behalf of the human race."[10] Instead of charging the United States with blasphemy, religious officials have focused mostly on the violations of the specific norms of the just-war tradition, and it is possible to set out four of the violations here:

Just cause

Catholic social teaching recognizes as just causes self-defense and humanitarian intervention on behalf of human rights. There can be *preemptive* strikes if an attack is imminent, but no "preventive war," that is,

8. "Operation Enduring Freedom"; Lampman, "Crusade After All?"

9. Walzer, *Just and Unjust Wars*.

10. Allen, "As Vatican Calls for Peace."

there can be no attack on another entity to prevent an attack that *might* take place some time in the more-distant future. On this the Vatican is clear. Cardinal Joseph Ratzinger, before he was made Pope Benedict XVI, said unequivocally, "The concept of preventive war does not appear in the catechism."[11] U.S. representatives sent the neoconservative Michael Novak to try to change the mind of the Vatican, but the Vatican was not persuaded. Novak says that he is following the just-war tradition, and that his view of the 2003 conflict with Iraq "has nothing to do with any new theory of 'preventive war.'" After examining the specifics of the possibility of an Iraqi attack on the United States, however, Novak warns: "Those who judge that the risk [of such an attack] is low and therefore allow Saddam to remain in power will bear a horrific responsibility if they *guessed wrong.*"[12] What sentences like these indicated to the Vatican, however, was that, for Novak, the use of armed force is indeed a question about what Iraq *might possibly* do, about "guessing," and not about imminent threat. In other words, Novak's program involves the engagement of preventive war, regardless of the name the action is given.

Last resort

From our argument so far, it is evident that preventive war violates not only the criterion of just cause but also the criterion of last resort. All nonviolent means of conflict resolution must be exhausted before resort to force. At the core of this criterion is the idea that war is not (despite what the architect of modern war, Carl von Clausewitz, claimed) merely another form of political activity. From a moral standpoint, war is an aberration. John Paul II was clear on this point in his January 13, 2003, "Address to the Diplomatic Corps":

> What are we to say of the threat of war that could strike the people of Iraq, the land of the prophets, a people already sorely tried by more than 12 years of embargo? War is never just another means that one can choose to employ for settling differences between nations. As the Charter of the United Nations Organization and international law itself remind us, war cannot be decided upon,

11. Ibid.

12. Novak, "Argument that War Against Iraq is Just," 593 and 596; italics added. For a fuller critique of Novak on this point, see Whitmore. "Reception of Catholic Approaches," 493–521.

even as a matter of ensuring the common good, except as the very last option and in accordance with very strict conditions.[13]

Legitimate Authority

John Paul II's reference to the international law and the United Nations also indicates that only a duly representative body can declare war. As the orthodox Catholic news source *Comunione e Liberazione* reported, then-Cardinal Ratzinger said about the 2003 engagement with Iraq, "Decisions like this should be made by the community of nations, by the UN, and not by an individual power."[14] The papal "foreign minister," Jean-Louis Tauran, concurred: "If the international community were to judge the recourse to force be opportune and proportionate, this should take place on the basis of a decision made within the framework of the United Nations."[15]

Reasonable Chance of Success

The Bush administration's rhetoric about the Iraq war often presupposes that persons who oppose it are naïve and uninformed about international relations and the demands of war. However, from early on, it has been evident that it is the administration that has been naïve. American fighting forces have been so underdeployed that anywhere from one-third to one-half of our soldiers have been reservists, "citizen soldiers," whose charter does not include fighting in extended engagements. Moreover, now as many as twenty-five thousand "corporate warriors"—soldiers hired by private companies for protection—work for as many as eighty companies in Iraq to carry out duties normally given to the military. Such corporate warriors constitute 16 percent of the coalition's total forces. Why? Retired general Jay Garner comments, "The gut of the problem is that the [U.S.] force is too small." Andrew Bearpark, the director of operations of the Coalition Provisional Authority, the governing body of the American-led occupation, adds, "The military just hadn't provided enough numbers."[16] The criterion of reasonable chance of success stipulates that there must be some chance of victory and of a return to peace, or else the violence

13. John Paul II, "Address to the Diplomatic Corps."
14. Brunelli, "No to 'Preventive War.'"
15. Ibid.
16. Bergner, "Other Army," 32.

and bloodshed are gratuitous. Even if one were to grant all of the other moral presuppositions of the administration, such as the Iraq war's just cause, this fact has remained: the administration has waged the Iraq war stupidly (the nicer but insufficiently direct word is "imprudently"), and in the just-war tradition, fighting stupidly is immoral because it causes unnecessary loss of human life.

More could be said about the morality of the war, including about the treatment of detainees, but what has already been said should be sufficient to indicate that U.S. engagement in the war goes against Church teaching as interpreted by the very highest of ecclesial authorities. It is important to add two points, however. First, neoconservative Catholics have tried to create space for their position by saying that they are simply making different applications of the just-war principles, and thus different but legitimate prudential judgments. However, the range of legitimate prudential judgment is not infinite, otherwise the just-war principles would be meaningless. Michael Novak's argument for preventive war under a different name is an attempt to appear as if he is simply making a different but legitimate prudential judgment. It is important to call him on this ruse. Second, Church authorities have given qualified approval of the war in Afghanistan. This qualified approval is important to note, because neoconservatives have taken Vatican opposition to the Iraq war as evidence that the Vatican is pacifist. On this point, the neoconservatives are once again wrong, as the Vatican's qualified support for counterterrorism activities indicates.[17]

When we move from international politics to domestic economics, George W. Bush does not fare any better. During the post–World War II years (approximately 1945 to 1973), the United States witnessed significant economic growth, and the percentage of American people in poverty declined dramatically. Beginning in the early seventies, economic production stagnated, and the percentage of people in poverty began to rise. The only sustained drop in the percentage of people in poverty during this time was during the 1990s. The only period in recent U.S. history that has witnessed a rise in the poverty rate during a period of significant growth in production has been the period of George W. Bush's presidency. In 2003 there was a 12 percent increase in productivity. However, real wages were stagnant or even declining. The *Wall Street Journal* reported

---

17. John Paul II, "No Peace without Justice, No Justice without Forgiveness."

that even though there was a 1.9 percent increase in wages, the consumer price index went up 3.3 percent, meaning a net loss for American families. Between 2000 and 2003, according to the *Journal*, the median household income fell by $1,500 or 3.4 percent.[18] During the same period, out-of-pocket medical expenses went up 49 percent for the American family, to $2,412. In the meantime, the rates of poverty also went up. In 2000, 11.3 percent of Americans were in poverty, according to official measures. The Census Bureau reports that by 2003, this number had climbed to 12.5 percent (and to 13.1 percent in 2004). In 2003 the percentage of children in poverty—17.6 percent—was the highest in ten years. Also in 2003, the number of people living without medical insurance jumped 1.5 million to reach 45 million people.[19]

With increased productivity, where is the income from this productivity going? Between the last quarter of 2001 and 2003, corporate profits went up 42 percent, according to the *Wall Street Journal*. The newspaper also reports that compensation for Wall Street executives went up 16 percent in 2003. However, the *Journal* is most descriptive when it tracks U.S. consumer patterns:

> The resulting two-tier recovery is showing up in vivid detail in the way Americans are spending money. Hotel revenue was up 11% (in 2003) at luxury and upscale chains . . . At the five-star Broadmoor Hotel in Colorado Springs, $600-a-night suites are sold out every day through mid-October . . . At high-end Bulgari stores, meanwhile, consumers are gobbling up $5,000 Astrale gold and diamond "cocktail rings" made for the right hand . . . Neiman Marcus Group, Inc., flourishing on sales of pricey items like $500 Manolo Blahnik shoes, had a 13.5% year-over-year sales rise . . . At Payless Shoe-Source, which sells items like $10.99 pumps, June sales were 1% *below* a year earlier.[20]

In short, increased productivity has not led to better well-being for poorer or even average Americans because, according to the fiscally conservative *Journal* (we are not talking about *Mother Jones* here), the well-off are getting more and spending it on themselves.

18. Hilsenrath and Freeman, "Two-Track Economy."

19. DeNavas-Walt et al., *Income, Poverty, and Health Insurance Coverage in the United States*.

20. Hilsenrath and Freeman, "Two-Track Economy" (italics added).

This turn of events is not by accident but is rather the result of policy. George W. Bush instituted tax reforms in both 2001 and 2003. According to Dean Maki, an economist at J. P. Morgan Chase, and formerly of the Federal Reserve, the top quintile of Americans got 77 percent of the 2003 tax cuts and 50 percent of the 2001 cuts.[21]

Catholic social teaching has long demonstrated a deep concern with the well-being of the poor. It has also decried the excessive gap between the rich and the poor, and not simply because of the conditions of the poor. The gathering up and hording of more and more consumer goods is itself a deep moral problem. Pope John Paul II's words are pointed:

> Side-by-side with the miseries of underdevelopment, themselves unacceptable, we find ourselves up against a form of superdevelopment, equally inadmissible, because like the former it is contrary to what is good and to true happiness. This superdevelopment, which consists in the excessive availability of every kind of material goods for the benefit of certain social groups, easily makes people slaves of "possession" and immediate gratification, with no other horizon than the multiplication or continual replacement of things already owned with others still better . . .
>
> All of us experience firsthand the effects of this blind submission to pure consumerism: in the first place a crass materialism, and at the same time a radical dissatisfaction, because one quickly learns that the more one possesses the more one wants, while deeper aspirations remain unsatisfied and perhaps even stifled.[22]

One could go on to address more issues, but the above is sufficient to indicate that the difference between the policies of George W. Bush and the teaching of the Catholic Church are so vastly different that the case for not having voted for Bush is a strong one.

---

21. Ibid.

22. John Paul II, *Solicitudo Rei Socialis*, par. 28. Catholic neoconservative Michael Novak charges that the attention to the rich/poor gap is "improper" and that John Paul II refers to the gap only "metaphorically." For the charge of "improper," see Lay Commission on Catholic Social Teaching and the U.S. Economy. *Toward the Future: Catholic Social Thought and the U.S. Economy*, 49. Novak was the primary drafter of the "Lay Commission" document. On "metaphorically," see Novak, *Catholic Ethic and the Spirit of Capitalism*, 152.

John Kerry

The main difficulty with the candidacy of John Kerry, and with the Democratic Party generally, was that the lack of a coherent and robust worldview reduced the presidential campaign to calculations of what was necessary to win. This reduction of the campaign into a battle to win was evident when Democratic insiders and pundits decided (on what basis it is unclear, given that Bill Clinton was at first a long shot to win the presidency) that the early primary leader, Howard Dean, "could not win" the presidential election.[23] The mood among Democrats was reflected in the bumper sticker, "Anyone but Bush." Largely because of his campaign war chest, John was judged to be that "anyone." As it turned out, he could not win either. In large part, he did not win precisely because of the public perception that while running for the Democratic nomination and for the presidency, he changed his policy positions simply as tactical moves. Bush boosters brandished orange footwear they called "Kerry flip-flops" as a sign of his lack of conviction.

If simply a matter of public perception, then the problem with John Kerry would be of another and lesser kind. The small extent of Kerry's problem is what the Democratic Party tried to convey after the election. They claimed that they simply "failed to get the message out." However, examination of Kerry's long-term positions on U.S. engagement with Iraq tells a different story. In January 1991, after Iraq invaded Kuwait, Kerry was one of the few senators who voted against authorizing U.S. engagement. In his words, "it is a vote about war because whether or not the president exercises his power, we will have no further say after this vote."[24] His vote was a concern about legitimate authority. However, in October 2002 and after 9/11, Kerry supported the second U.S. engagement, despite the fact that Iraq had not attacked another country this time, and despite the fact of much international opposition to an armed engagement.

In just-war terms, there was not a just cause for the second Iraq engagement, and far less (if any) legitimate authority to attack. The only circumstances that had changed between 1991 and 2002 that might have accounted for Kerry's change in policy position in the intervening years then, are the intensity of public opinion about security threats given 9/11, and Kerry's own presidential candidacy. On August 9, 2004, John Kerry

23. Wilgoren, "2004 Campaign: The Former Governor."
24. Kuhn, "Kerry's Top Ten Flip-Flops."

argued for his vote in supporting George W. Bush on Iraq, saying, in direct opposition to his 1991 vote, "I believe that it was the right authority for a president to have."[25] He muted this position by saying that he would have fought the present war differently from the way Bush was fighting it, but given the dramatic shifts in his understanding of just cause and legitimate authority, it is hard to read the "would-have-fought-the-war-differently" comment as anything other than a strategic campaign adjustment once the fighting started going badly.

John Kerry has demonstrated a number of similar changes on domestic policy—from affirmative action (which in 1992 he called "inherently limited and divisive" but supported in his presidential campaign) to Bush's "No Child Left Behind Act" (which he voted for but campaigned against).[26] In each case, the change appears to have been not the result of careful reexamination of the issue itself (I consider such willingness to reexamine an issue to be a political virtue), but rather the result of the pressure of public opinion.

It might be good, then, to examine the one issue where Kerry has appeared to be consistent—abortion—to examine the fit of his candidacy with Catholic teaching. I say "has appeared to be" because, as we will see, the evidence on abortion points toward the shaping of a position meant to make him politically viable, despite whatever inconsistencies it may contain.

Kerry first set out his position on abortion as early as 1972 (that is, before *Roe v. Wade*) when he told the *Lowell Sun*: "On abortion, I myself, by belief and upbringing, am opposed to abortion but as a legislator, as one who is called on to pass a law, I would find it very difficult to legislate on something God himself has not seen fit to make clear to all people on this earth . . . And I think, therefore, with a sense of justice in mind that one has to leave the question of abortion between a woman and her conscience and her doctor."[27] The reasoning of his position was the same in the second presidential debate in October 2004. "First of all, I cannot tell you how deeply I respect the belief about life and when it begins. I'm a Catholic—raised a Catholic. I was an altar boy. Religion has been a huge part of my life . . . But I can't take what is an article of faith and legislate

25. Quoted in "John Kerry on Faith."
26. See Kuhn, "Kerry's Top Ten Flip-Flops."
27. Quoted in VandeHei, "Events Forcing Abortion Issue on Kerry."

it for someone who does not share that article of faith."[28] By his reference to his being raised Catholic, Kerry intends to convey that he is in agreement with the judgment of official Church teaching that human life begins at conception. This intention is clear in a July 2004 interview in the *Telegraph Herald* of Dubuque, Iowa: "I oppose abortion personally. I don't like abortion. I believe that life begins at conception."[29] However, his opposition to limits on abortion led NARAL Pro-Choice America (formerly the National Abortion Rights Action League) to give him a 100 percent rating for his votes on the issue since 1997.

From a Catholic perspective, the problem with Kerry's policy position is that while Church teaching does make a *distinction* between the moral law and human law—not all things that are immoral ought also be illegal—it does not make so great a *separation* between the two as to back a blanket statement that no law can be passed to restrict the taking of human life. Kerry's "personally opposed, but . . ." position depends on an utter *separation* of public and private that finds its primary home in contractarian thought: one contracts into "public" arrangements so as to protect one's "private" activity.[30] Rights protect these zones of privacy. Catholic social teaching, however, begins with an understanding of the person as social. The family is the "first society." The key Catholic distinction is between society and the state, so that, like contractarianism, there are zones of activity protected from direct state involvement. Again, not all immoral activities ought to be illegal. However, given the gravity of taking human life, the summary statement that no limits can be placed on the activity in the case of unborn life is bizarre from a Catholic standpoint, and depends on a complete separation rather than a distinction between the moral and the legal.[31]

The question that arises is what would lead to such a strange, even (and I use this word advisedly) grotesque campaign position that combines the claims that (1) abortion is the taking of human life, and (2)

28. Quoted in "John Kerry on Faith."

29. Quoted in Fisher, "Kerry Says He Believe Life Starts at Conception."

30. The most fully articulated defense of this position by Catholic politicians is Cuomo, "Religious Belief and Public Morality." Cuomo gave this speech at the University of Notre Dame in 1984. Geraldine Ferraro followed this line of reasoning during her vice-presidential campaign in 1984.

31. For fuller accounts of this critique, see Whitmore, "What Would John Courtney Murray Say?"; and Kenneth L. Woodward, "Catholics, Politics & Abortion."

that there ought to be no legal restrictions on abortion? It is hard not to come to the conclusion that political forces once again shape Kerry's ultimate position more than moral principles do, and this for a couple reasons, both of which disclose inconsistencies in the development of that position.

First, on other political issues, ones that align with the Democratic Party, Kerry does not hesitate not only to make a link but a direct connection between his faith and his policy. On July 6, 2004, in a speech to the African Methodist Episcopal (AME) convention, he said, "We should never separate our highest beliefs and values from our treatment of one another and our conduct of other people's business." He clarified what counted as "other people's business" in the third presidential debate on October 13, 2004: "I think that everything you do in public life has to be guided by your faith, affected by your faith . . . That's why I fight against poverty. That's why I fight to clean up the environment and protect this earth. That's why I fight for equality and justice . . . President Kennedy in his inaugural address told us that here on earth God's work must be truly our own. And that's what we have to—I think that's the test of public service."[32] In short, when the policy issue shifts to one that the Democrats support, Kerry changes his reasoning on the relationship between faith and politics.

Second, Kerry's position is shaped by the fact that it is virtually impossible for a pro-life Democrat to get the party nomination for president. Twice Kerry has either voted for or indicated that he would vote for some restrictions on abortion. In 1997, he voted for a bill that would have banned most postviability abortions. Moreover, during the 2004 presidential campaign, he did say that he would support a "partial-birth" abortion ban if there were an exception for the life and health of the mother. However, the first vote was in 1997, well before the campaign; during his presidential campaign, Kerry never mentioned his vote for the ban even when specifically talking about abortion. Kerry's seeming stance in opposition to "partial-birth" abortion is meaningless because, as he knows, pro-life politicians would never back a "health-of-the-mother" exception,

32. Quoted in "John Kerry on Faith." With the abortion issue in mind, Kerry added the caveat that religion should issue in action, "but without transferring it in any official way to other people" (third presidential debate, October 13, 2004). However, when he refers in the same quote to his record on poverty and the environment, it is precisely policy—that is, official—action that he is talking about.

given the seeming infinite expansiveness of the concept of "health." In the meantime, Kerry opposes the restriction.

Recent comments and moves by the Democratic Party appear to indicate some flexibility on abortion, but it remains the case that a presidential hopeful needs to maintain high NARAL marks. Hilary Clinton makes her call for pro-choice/pro-life cooperation in aiding women with unintended pregnancies only within the context of a stout affirmation on her support of no legal restrictions on abortion; and although the national party recruited pro-life Democrat Robert Casey Jr. to run for Pennsylvania senator, there are no indications that such flexibility will extend to presidential candidates. This is odd because that very flexibility is the result of Democratic perceptions that an unqualified pro-choice platform was a significant factor in the loss of the presidential election in 2004. A *New York Times* article did comment, "National party leaders heavily recruited Mr. Casey to enter this race (for senator only), despite his long opposition to abortion rights, because, quite simply, they thought he could win."[33] It would be interesting to see what would happen to the positions of Democratic presidential hopefuls if it became the party's received wisdom that it could not win any *national* election while remaining unqualifiedly pro-choice.

In sum, then, it seems that what at first appears to be an internally consistent position on abortion—("personally opposed, but no legal limits") runs into inconsistency both in the way that Kerry relates religion to political life (abortion is the only issue where the two are utterly separated) and in the way that his policy on abortion itself (at times backing restrictions, before the presidential campaign, but in practice opposing all restrictions, during the campaign). My own interpretation is that the 1972 Kerry opposed restrictions based on principle, and that the 1997 Kerry, on principle, began to change his mind, but that the 2004 Kerry wanted the presidency and was willing to apply to abortion a completely different theory of the relationship between religion and politics than he applied to other issues, in order to make his campaign position on abortion appear firm to Democratic insiders, thus assuring them that despite previous lapses, he was going to hold the party line on this issue. This is the only sense that I can make of the development and logic of Kerry's position on abortion.

33. Toner, "To Democrats Hungry for Senate." See also Boyer, "Right to Choose," 52–61.

∽

Given the extent to which candidates Bush and Kerry each missed the mark on both foreign and domestic issues, I decided, after much careful deliberation, not to vote in the 2004 presidential election. My argument is not that of Ralph Nader—that there are no important differences between the candidates. My calculus is a different one: is the distance between Catholic teaching and the candidate nearest to it greater than the distance between the candidates? The candidate closest to Catholic teaching will vary depending on the issue, but almost without exception the gap between the two candidates is less that the distance of either candidate from Catholic teaching. I ask the bishops and "Faithful Citizenship": how bad do the choices have to be before the decision not to vote is the right one?

The bishops themselves give us some guidance on the matter in their 1983 pastoral latter, *The Challenge of Peace: God's Promise and Our Response*. There, they distinguish between fundamental principles and their applications. All persons—even those who are not Catholic—must adhere to the fundamental principles of the moral life. The bishops are clear on this distinction:

> Indeed, we stress here at the beginning that not every statement in this letter has the same moral authority. At times we reassert universally binding moral principles (e.g., noncombatant immunity and proportionality). . . . Again, at other times we apply moral principles to specific cases. When making applications of these principles we realize—and we wish readers to recognize—that prudential judgments are involved based on specific circumstances which can change or which can be interpreted differently by people of good will.[34]

It would seem, then, that whenever a candidate diverges from what church officials say not just on the application of the principle to a specific case, but on the principle itself, it is legitimate, and even called for, to not vote for that candidate. George Bush's stance on the Iraq war as reflected in his statements and actions, in my judgment goes even beyond divergence on the principle to outright idolatry. It violates the first and second commandments. Even in the Vatican's more restricted criticism, Bush is undercutting the just war criteria of just cause and last resort by introduc-

34. United States Conference of Catholic Bishops, *Challenge of Peace*, paragraphs 9–10.

ing the idea of "preventive war." The economic analogue to political rights as articulated in the just war criteria is economic rights—for instance, the rights to a living wage, health care, and housing. George Bush rejects the very idea of economic rights, and this is reflected in his economic policy as detailed above. John Kerry's case is different, if only in the fact that on both foreign and domestic policy he does not seem to have firm principles—at least ones that he is willing to translate consistently into public life—and this is indicated in his shifting around on Iraq and his grotesque logic on abortion. Bush and Kerry are both not simply wrong on foreign and domestic policy, but wrong at very fundamental levels that are impervious to substantive change.

The question for any ensuing election is whether the candidates fit under the same analysis. In this regard, all three of the remaining candidates—Hillary Clinton, John McCain, and Barack Obama—are far from fully acceptable. McCain is not idolatrous like George Bush is, but still upholds the idea of "preventive war." It is unclear as of yet whether McCain's economic policies will be much different than Bush's. Neither Obama nor Clinton tries to truss up their abortion positions by saying that they believe that the embryo is a human person like Kerry does. In other words, they uphold the idea that there is no direct killing of innocent persons; they just do not think or pretend to think that the embryo is a person. Still, they show no signs of allowing an interpretation of Roe v. Wade that sets any limits on abortion. Like McCain in relation to Bush on the war, Obama and Clinton are wrong, just not as perversely wrong as Kerry on abortion. Given that Clinton has been weak either way on the war and, in my judgment, too aligned with the economically strong, that leaves Obama and McCain as the most viable options from a Catholic standpoint. Whether they continue to be depends on what they say and do in the remainder of the election.

The electoral college structure also informs my decision not to vote. Historically, the Electoral College arose out of concern about the dangers of "mass rule." It was a brokered compromise between parliamentary and democratic systems. In many states, such as my own state of Indiana, it is a structure of nonparticipation: given the heavily Republican nature of the state, my vote, regardless of which party I vote for, has literally no weight. My concern here is that the "get-out-the-vote" campaign, as important as it is, can be a sop for what is really nonparticipation, and this in two ways: votes really do not count as much as the "get-out-the-vote" campaign implies, and the campaign can be heard as suggesting that once people do vote, they have adequately done their civic duty.

The actual *presidential* campaigns themselves know that my vote does not count, as is evidenced in their stumping and spending patterns. Both candidates and their monies were noteworthy by their absence from my state. In the last month of the campaign, the candidates spent $237 million in advertising. Two hundred twenty-nine million dollars of that money was spent in thirteen states. Twenty-three states saw *no* spending in presidential-campaign advertising during this time. (In contrast, both Obama and Clinton are campaigning heavily in Indiana in the 2008 Democratic primary, where, unlike with the Electoral College, it is not "winner take all" and therefore all votes do in fact count.) The Electoral College is deeply antidemocratic.[35] If the bishops want to get the vote out, critique of the Electoral College is where they should start.

III. What Remains of Civic Obligation?

The reflections so far lead to my final section. The specific duty not to vote in a particular election does not exempt us from the duty of solidarity. In fact, viewed rightly, the decision not to vote *is* an act of solidarity towards the common good. The question is, what other obligations remain?

Before going to these other obligations, one question is whether the presence of alternative parties and write-in candidacies keep intact the obligation to vote in the presidential election. Here my argument is that, at present, the American system is structured so that third parties are almost guaranteed electoral failure in presidential elections. Therefore, the presence of the parties as if they are electorally significant (though they may be significant in other ways) on the presidential level (though they may be significant on other levels of government) is misleading. Voting for or writing in candidates may make us feel good, but at the expense of our coming to terms with just how dysfunctional the electoral system is.

Two obligations remain after not voting on the presidential level: The first is to vote on the other levels of government—or at least to undertake discernment on each electoral level. The obligation not to vote in one election does not spill over to another election. The second obliga-

35. On the effect of the Electoral College on spending and voting patterns, see Hertzberg, "Count 'Em," 27–28. On how little impact individual votes have on the outcome of elections, see Dubner and Levitt, "Why Vote?" 30–32.

tion is to contribute to the common good in nonelectoral ways. Again, the "get-out-the-vote" campaign makes voting seem the major part of the duty to solidarity, when voting is only one aspect of what should be a multifaceted commitment.

I conclude by picking up where I began: the issue of the informed conscience. I have researched the teaching—or rather the lack of teaching—of Catholic social teaching in Catholic colleges and universities.[36] The bishops speak as if the laity's consciences have already received adequate formation in the tradition. Such an assumption is ill founded. The bishops' first obligation is not to tell the laity to vote, but to ensure that the whole of the Catholic tradition is in fact consistently taught in Catholic schools, so that the laity indeed know the tradition. This is the main precondition for Catholics to make informed and conscientious electoral decisions. Teach the tradition well; then the idea of a "Catholic vote" might mean something more than a demographic that has to be watched by presidential hopefuls.

Postscript: I am yet undecided about whether I will vote in the 2008 election, pending a hearing of the views of the candidates.

36. On this point, see Whitmore, "Teaching and Living Practical Reasoning," 1–36; and "In the Mission or On the Margins," 73–86.

7

Voting With Our Lives: Ongoing Conversations along the Path to Pentecostal Faithfulness

Paul Alexander

I want to vote. I want to change the world and make it a better place. I mean, just think about it: the world is full of poverty, starvation, famine, disease, violence, abuse, corruption, exploitation, rape, murder, and greed. So if someone is going to argue against voting, they had better have a very good plan for doing something about this messed-up world—or admit they don't care, or that nothing can be done about it. I care, and I think that something can be done about it.

And I'm a follower of Jesus of Nazareth. In fact, I'm a Holy-Spirit–baptized, tongue-talking student of the Messiah. Jesus has messed up a lot in my life; for instance, I have learned from him that God doesn't want me to use violence to make the world a better place. I will for the rest of my life be learning how to embody this, so that I can bless this world that God loves, but I'm convinced it's true. And I'm convinced that God does indeed love the world and desires less sin and more love than there is now. So, is voting a legitimate strategy for faithful Christians to use to witness to the kingship of God? Is voting a legitimate strategy to help redeem the world right here and now where people are really suffering, and where bad stuff is happening all the time? Is voting a legitimate strategy to reduce sin and violence, to increase the peace, and to glorify God—to be the church we're called to be?

It has a lot to do with how we define "voting," and how we define "church." If voting is inherently violent and coercive, then there is no question that it is not an option for us to use, since Christians are not supposed to coerce or force people to follow our understanding of God's will. But if voting is a form of persuasion and argument rather than a form of violence, then voting may be okay in limited circumstances; Christians are certainly encouraged to speak about our faith and about our hope for the world.

The English word *vote* comes from the Latin *votum*, which means "a vow, wish, promise, or dedication." So everybody votes. We all wish for something. We make promises, and we dedicate ourselves to some truth, cause, hope, or goal. A decent definition of *vote* is "a formal expression of opinion or choice, either positive or negative, made by an individual or group of individuals."[1] I would like to suggest that our lives—the very ways we live day by day—are formal expressions of our opinions and choices. If I buy sweatshop-free sneakers or tell the motel staff not to worry about cleaning my room, then I am voting—I am expressing my opinion and choice about how I wish the world would be. I am also helping to create it. Children vote for and against toys and playtime activities. People in prison vote when they choose whether to read or exercise during their free time. Any time human beings have options and have the ability to participate or refrain, we are voting and bringing about a different world than the one that existed before our vote.

We vote every day. We choose food, clothing, friends, enemies, activities, goals, TV shows, music, and books. We choose the sources of our news and information, or whether we even bother accessing news. A journal of what we do or not do with our time, and what we do or not do with our money is our voting record. Hours playing basketball, days playing with children, weeks in Palestine, months reading, years teaching, a night in jail for civil disobedience; these are our votes.

But the question posed to us is whether or not, and to what extent, we participate in organized elections in a society with a limited number of options—options between which we supposedly have to choose in order to be conscientious and responsible citizens. These options include propositions and resolutions, members of the school board and the city council, mayors, county commissioners, state officials, governors, congresspersons, presidents; and pastors, deacons, and elders. Perhaps we should vote on single-issue propositions or for pastors but not for presidents since, for instance, presidents are commanders in chief of military forces, who promise to defend America with violence. Perhaps if the result of a vote would be enforced with violence, then maybe that vote should be off limits; but if we won't call in the militia or the courts to enforce our

1. "Vote," *Dictionary.com*.

vote for our church elders, then maybe that voting is okay. Defining voting is one part of the discussion and will not get us as far down the road as we need to go; having a better understanding of the church will. Since I'm a Pentecostal, and we have a radical heritage, I'll briefly resurrect some early twentieth-century teachings about Christian citizenship and then move on to some theological and practical reflections.

A Bit of Pentecostal History

Reading early Pentecostals inspired me because I realized that nationalism and the body of God form a lethal combination. This combination led me to think of one of the most violent games ever invented, and one of my favorites, an entertainment that unites emperor and clergy, military and peasantry in an attempt to defeat the enemy and to perpetuate one's own kingdom. The game, of course, is chess. The bishops, the representatives of the people of God, stand closest to the king and queen. They are closer than the cavalry (the knights) or the siege towers (the rooks). The church is entangled in the empire, seeking first its kingdom, striking at an angle for the color of its national kin. Chess is a great game, but it's a rather dangerous ecclesiology and practice.

The majority of early Pentecostals believed that "Christians' fundamental allegiance should never be lodged with the state since the state was an earthly fabrication. Like the Tower of Babel, the state signaled human presumption at best, the enthronement of godlessness, immorality, greed, and violence at worst."[2] Pentecostals often argued that "the United States did not deserve Christians' allegiance," and that "no state, including the United States, had ever been Christian."[3]

Early Pentecostals preached that the greatest spiritual evil of the age was "immoderate patriotism" that led to "national sectarianism,"[4] and that Fourth-of-July celebrations were wastes of God's money.[5] Pentecostals also bravely questioned democracy, viewing it as a political scheme by which humans could accomplish their prideful goals. They called democracy the political system condemned in Daniel, "rule of the

2. Wacker, *Heaven Below*, 217.

3. Ibid., 218.

4. H. Musgrave Reade. *Trust*, November 1917, 13, quoted in Wacker, *Heaven Below*, 218.

5. Levi Lupton. *News Acts*, July 4, 1906, 8, quoted in Wacker, *Heaven Below*, 219.

people with God left out," control by "popular passion"; so they concluded that "democracy will not save the world, Republicanism will not bring the Millennium."[6] Charles Parham (the first teacher of the doctrine that praying in tongues is the evidence of being filled with the Spirit) taught that Pentecostals should not vote, and that "fighting by sword or ballot arouses all the carnal there is in people."[7] A. J. Tomlinson (founder of the Church of God, Cleveland, Tennessee) vowed never to vote for anyone except Jesus.[8] Many Pentecostals put ecclesiology above nationalism and voted with their lives for Jesus Christ as king. They relied on the body politics of Christian community rather than on the government.

William Burton McCafferty (an Assemblies of God pastor and professor) preached that "our citizenship is not of this world, our citizenship is in heaven [Phil 3:20] . . . We belong to the Kingdom of God and the Kingdom of God and the kingdoms of this world are not allied."[9] The FBI charged that C. H. Mason (founder of the predominantly African American Church of God in Christ) "openly advised against registration [for the draft] and made treasonable and seditious remarks against the United States government."[10] The FBI believed that Mason could be convicted of treason, of obstructing the draft, and of giving aid and comfort to the enemy. Both the FBI and the War Department opened files on Mason and on the Church of God in Christ, and Mason interviewed with several agents. The *Vicksburg Post* ran an article claiming that Mason's preaching to resist the draft had led to the state adjutant general to declare that it was virtually impossible to get blacks in Lexington to respond to the draft.[11]

Frank Bartleman, a prominent and widely published early Pentecostal leader, condemned specific sins of every nation, from England and America to Germany, Russia, Italy, France, and Japan, declaring that "we speak without fear or favor. . . .We favor no country."[12] His Christian citizenship provided the distance that he needed to tell the truth about the

6. Wacker, *Heaven Below*, 219.

7. Parham. *Apostolic Faith*, March 1912, 2, quoted in Wacker *Heaven Below*, 222. For a theological explanation of this see Yoder, "Christian Case for Democracy"; and Yoder, "Civil Religion in America."

8. Tomlinson, *Answering the Call of God*, 10, quoted in Wacker, *Heaven Below*, 222.

9. McCafferty, "Should Christians Go To War?" 1.

10. Agent M. M. Schaumburger to Bureau of Investigation, September 24, 1917.

11. Kornweibel, "Race and Conscientious Objection in World War I," 61.

12. Bartleman, "European War," 3.

sins of all nations, and he certainly wasn't voting for any politicians of any nation. Lest anyone question his lack of loyalty to the government of the United States, Bartleman provided his attitude toward national fidelity: "Patriotism has been fanned into a flame. . . . The religious passion has been invoked, and the national gods called upon for defense in each case . . . What blasphemy!"[13] He continued his tirade against nationalism, defended the outcasts, and added a call to repentance.

> It is not worth while for Christians to wax warm in patriotism over this world's situation. . . . American capitalists, leaders and manufacturers are as deep in the mud as the others. . . . [Germans] are in the wrong sometimes also, and they are likely to stand by their country, right or wrong. England will do that also. America will do the same thing. . . . There is not principle enough in any of these countries to overcome that.[14]

Bartleman believed that "there is no righteous nation in the earth today" and blamed "nominal Christianity" (the opposite of radical Pentecostal Christianity) for the disastrous atrocities that America had perpetrated.

> We have killed off about all of our American Indians. What we have not killed outright we have starved. . . . We have stolen the land from the North American Indians. . . . Our wrong to the black people was avenged in blood. What will the next be?[15]

Stanley Frodsham believed that "when one comes into that higher kingdom and becomes a citizen of that 'holy nation' (1 Pet 2:9), the things that pertain to earth should forever lose their hold, even that natural love for the nation where one happened to be born, and loyalty to the new King should swallow up all other loyalties."[16] Charles Parham criticized American Christians for bowing to the "Moloch God, Patriotism" and believed the nation was not worth fighting for and that it would "end with a dictator and a final fall . . . in which the government, the rich and the churches will be on one side and the masses on the other."[17] Some Pentecostals saw the slavery, genocide, and greed of the American experi-

13. Ibid.

14. Bartleman, "What Will the Harvest Be?" 1.

15. Ibid., 2.

16. Frodsham, "Our Heavenly Citizenship," 3.

17. Parham, Sarah. *Life of Charles F. Parham*, 274, quoted in Wacker, *Heaven Below*, 218.

ment quite clearly and attempted to speak prophetically about it. Frank Bartleman even declared that America should "pluck the stars from its flag and instate dollar signs in their place."[18] These Pentecostals were not the bishops allied with the kings or voting for the presidents, using the peasants on the front lines to advance the empire.

Prophetic, Patriotic, Pentecostal Pacifism; or, Spirit-Empowered, Nonnationalistic Nonviolence

First-generation Pentecostals prophetically protested violence and nationalism, and they critiqued voting as an unnecessary and unfaithful participation in the system. They combined the practice of biblical interpretation with social and political analysis. They highlighted the biblical themes of justice, peace, mission, the kingdom of God, and Spirit empowerment. These contrasted with their analysis of the situation of the world: injustice, war, and national arrogance. American Pentecostals have the heritage and theological resources to enable both a faithful ecclesiology and a contemporary critique of nationalism and voting. Pentecostals and evangelicals should seek a postcritical reappropriation of this countercultural witness from their tradition, and I propose prophetic patriotic Pentecostal pacifism as a possible way forward.

The prophets of God name and expose the injustices and violence in all the nations of the world and among the people of God as well. *Vox populi* (the voice of the people) and *realpolitik* (pragmatic politics) do not determine their actions or their messages; they humbly and powerfully speak the words of God in a sinful world. Thus, they often experience popularity problems. The kings tortured Jeremiah, the empire crucified Jesus, and Dr. Martin Luther King Jr. fell to an assassin's bullet.

A cornerstone passage of Scripture for Pentecostals is Acts 2, part of which is a quotation from Joel: "In these last days I will pour out my Spirit upon all flesh. Your sons and your daughters will prophesy." To prophesy, even to be eschatologically driven, is not to predict the imminent end of all things. To prophesy is to have the courage of the biblical prophets to speak out loud in public about the idolatry of nation worship, about the hoarding of wealth at the expense of the poor, and about dependence on military strength and violence for security. This prophetic voice was one significant reason why both liberal and fundamentalist Christians

18. Bartleman, "European War," 3.

disliked Pentecostals in the early twentieth century. Pentecostals blamed compromising Christians for slavery, massacres, and war. The charismatic prophet today, if influenced by early Pentecostalism, would illuminate connections between the complicit church and the injustice and violence in the land. This places her in a dangerous tradition.

American Christians of almost every political type argue about who is the most patriotic. Antiwar folk say that the most patriotic action that supports the military and the nation is not to have invaded Iraq and to bring the troops home now (or soon). Those who support the war in Iraq say they themselves are the ones who are being patriotic by continuing the fight. Most Americans want to be considered patriots, and cherish the label. But the prophetic, politically radical Pentecostal Christian does not seek that title. Many early Pentecostals would have said, "You think I'm not patriotic? Perhaps your patriotism is worship of false gods." Nevertheless, *patriotism* is a powerful word and can perhaps be put to work within the Pentecostal prophetic tradition. Pentecostals are called to be citizens and patriots in the kingdom of God, a kingdom or *ethnos* that, according to Christian claims, transcends and outlasts all other kingdoms and nation-states. The permanence of the kingdom of God is an important biblical theme highlighted within Pentecostalism, and this is true freedom. This understanding of the kingdom of God enables an internationalism not captivated by or subordinated to any particular nation. Prophetic patriotic Pentecostals should be able to say again, "We speak without fear or favor, we favor no country."[19]

The majority of Pentecostals and charismatics in the world are not United States citizens. For instance, only 7 percent of the thirty-eight million Assemblies of God adherents are U.S. citizens. I appreciate this because the majority of white Pentecostals and charismatics in America practice nationalism and militarism.[20] Yet the passionate and articulate multiethnic voices in Pentecostal history show us resources within the "Spirit-filled church" that can provide more international and less violent ways of practicing Pentecostalism.

Pentecostals have a strong history of pacifism, though they shunned the word even when they were pacifists. They did not passively avoid conflict, and they did risk their lives for the gospel, but they rejected the

19. For a helpful analysis of distance and belonging, see Volf, *Exclusion and Embrace*, 35–55.

20. Alexander, "Spirit Empowered Peacemaking," 78–102.

belief that Christians should kill for their own safety or for the preserva-
tion of their nations. Prophetic, patriotic pacifism is nonnationalistic and
nonviolent, but it not as a position on nation or war per se. [21] Prophetic,
patriotic pacifism flows from a conviction that the peasant from Galilee,
Jesus of Nazareth, revealed the way of God to the world, *and* that the
Spirit of this God empowers the followers of Jesus to prophetically challenge idolatrous nationalism—nationalism that requires the sacrifice of
its enemies for the nation's own continued existence.

John Howard Yoder noted that early Pentecostal pacifism, "wrought
by the synergy of enthusiasm and prima facie biblicism . . . did not mature
into a solid ethical hermeneutic."[22] I agree and hope to rectify this, and I
am not the first to call for the restoration of pacifism among Pentecostals.[23]
Although for many years I was ashamed to call myself a Pentecostal, I
now recognize the necessity of emphasizing the enabling of the Spirit to
live (and perhaps to die) as prophetic, nonviolent citizens in the kingdom of God. Becoming a Christian pacifist has helped me appreciate my
Pentecostalism.

Pentecostals believe that God empowers followers of Jesus to witness faithfully. The book of Acts also says, "You will receive power when
the Holy Spirit comes upon you, and you will be my witnesses." I do not
advocate witnessing or missions in the form of colonialism, though this
is undoubtedly what many early Pentecostals had in mind, but I would
argue that a postcolonial Christian witness is both possible and necessary.
Radical Pentecostals who transcend and critique political parties must
rely on the Spirit of God for their sustenance. Public, prophetic witness
about justice and peace is good news for the poor, the weak, the rich, and
the powerful—though the rich and powerful may not receive the witness
as good news, and for this mission of spreading the good news, the Spirit's
wise leading and enabling are indispensable.

Spirit-empowered, nonnationalistic nonviolence advocates neither
withdrawal from society nor abdication of one's ethnicity or nationality,
but a thoroughly Christian relationship to all people. We should be truth
tellers who speak honestly about the good, the bad, the ugly, and the
beautiful in any nation.

---

21. See Cahill, *Love Your Enemies.*
22. Yoder, Foreword to *Pentecostal Pacifism,* iii–v.
23. See Shuman, "Pentecost and the End of Patriotism," 70–96.

We need to embody some aspects of Hispanic American Pentecostalism as described by Eldin Villafañe.[24] "In a real historical sense they [Hispanic Americans] are a pilgrim people. . . . Being a border people, no matter where we live, we must serve as a means of communication between the rich, overaffluent and misdeveloped world of the North, and the poor, exploited and also misdeveloped world of the South. This . . . requires that we continue to be bilingual and bicultural." I propose that the church be a humble, prophetic, transnational, nonviolent, and Spirit-empowered *ethnos* who lives and speaks God's counterintuitive will and way while being on the chessboard but not of the chessboard.

Now What?

But I still have questions about not voting. What about Dr. King and the voting-rights act? What about women getting the vote? It's hard for me to disagree with Dr. King's work to open opportunities for more people to effect change through voting. I love the civil rights movement and have been greatly influenced by Dr. King. But can we with clear consciences vote for any person who will do things that Jesus would not want us to do? I know it's crazy, but Jesus is about all I have. I say "about all" because I'm also supposed to be a part of a church that is indeed Jesus's body on earth. If God has a body, and we are it, then my wish, my voice, my life, my vote has to be completely in line with God's will—and electing people who will ignore the way of Jesus, as best I understand it, would be less than total allegiance to the king of all kings, the president of all presidents. If I abandon the democratic vote, then I have to have something else to dedicate myself to, something else to hope in for a more just and peaceful world. That's where the Spirit-empowered people of God come in: it's on us.

Presidents are elected every four years in the United States: that is, every 1,460 days. More than 122 million American citizens voted on November 2, 2004, in the presidential election. If the number of citizens who did something on one day to determine the presidency is multiplied by the number of days they live while that one president is in office, the total number of days f is more than 178 *billion* days of living. That's a lot of life lived by those who voted. The remaining 95 million Americans over the age of eighteen who did not vote lived a combined 140 billion days of life. What's the point?

24. Villafañe, *Liberating Spirit*, 89, 163, 165, 171, 198–99.

We are told to make our vote "count." In that statement I hear, "Make your life count." There's a lot more life to be lived than the thirty minutes I might spend voting for a president. I grant that what the president does is powerful and world changing, but it is not as powerful as what the church can be. And I think that voting for a president who practices and perpetuates actions not in line with my theology or ethics, (i.e., not in line with my faith[fulness]) is not necessary in order to be the Jesus-shaped, Spirit-empowered people of God that we are called to be. For presidential candidates, if they claim to be Christian, present different kinds and degrees of Christian unfaithfulness. Scripture encourages us to choose life; Scripture never tells us to choose the lesser of two evils. Maybe we should not vote when ours is a choice between the lesser of two bad choices. Nowhere in Scripture are we told to choose death or to choose the bad; we are to choose only life. If I do not have that option before me, then I choose life with my life. And that is certainly a vote.

I started this essay by saying that the world is hurting, I want to help, and voting seems like a way to do that. But if arguments against Christians voting are convincing, then we have to take very seriously the call to live our faith publicly, sacrificially, and controversially. I know that we are not called by God to coerce, dominate, and force our way. And maybe it's the Pentecostal in me, but I don't think we're called to passivity either. So that leaves us with only our trust that God's way of self-giving love that can be rejected—the kingdom that will never pass away—will be made manifest as we live faithfully. First Corinthians says that Jews want power, and Gentiles want wisdom—I want both (1 Cor 1: 18–31)! But all I have is a murdered God on a cross, Christ crucified, which is weak and stupid, both a stumbling block and foolishness. Abandoning voting, trusting God, and being the church seem weak and stupid to me; these options do not seem like a very good plan to help the world. Unless, of course, noncoercive love is the true grain of the universe. About the only way I can see the logic and power in it is to stay focused on the Galilean peasant's forgiving his enemies as they murdered him, to believe that his forgiveness really showed us something, to live faithfully and openly, and to hope for resurrection.

8

The Folly of Not Voting:
Reflections on the Incoherence of the Church

Tato Sumantri

Incoherent to the World

I decided in 1980 to abstain from presidential elections. However, the theological underpinnings of that decision have developed and coalesced over time. What began as an angry and frustrated declaration of "No, Jesus is Lord!" has, over time and discipleship, developed into a fuller understanding of Jesus the Servant King, of the cruciform nature of the kingdom of God, and of my participation in that kingdom. To that end, I find myself indebted to more people than I can possibly hope to remember and acknowledge. At the top of that heap stand my brothers and sisters of Church of the Servant King in Eugene, Oregon. It is only within the context of a community of believers, that is to say a church, that Scripture is understood, its meaning is refined, and ultimately faith and hope are lived out.

Not long ago my nephew asked me about Vernard Eller's *Christian Anarchy*. While trying to figure out his place in the world and his own identity, my nephew Randy has identified with the punk/anarchist crowd prevalent in the Portland, Oregon, area. Randy and I, through his teen years, have had quite a few conversations and even debates about politics, about the nation-state, and about the Iraq war. He has had no leanings at all toward Jesus, in spite of the fact that, and perhaps because, his dad is a pastor. For the most part, he saw a copy of *Christian Anarchy* on a book-shelf in my home during Thanksgiving dinner, and the title intrigued him. After our conversation, I found a copy for him and gave it to him as an early Christmas present. But in giving him the book, I warned him that it might make no sense to him whatsoever since Eller made claims to the lordship of Jesus.

In the same way that I warned my nephew Randy about Eller's *Christian Anarchy*, I appeal to brothers and sisters in Christ, and I make no appeal to the world at large. Everything that I believe, especially as what I believe pertains to such issues as my participation in the nation-state and nonviolence, takes root in the cross of Jesus and in my discipleship to Jesus. It is only in the context of discipleship to Jesus that anything that I have to say has any hope of coherence. I would further posit that outside the context of the cross of Jesus and discipleship to Jesus, everything I have to say becomes incoherent.

My History: Indonesia's Revolutions to the Carter Presidency

My story really cannot be told without stepping back a generation to talk about the history of Indonesia, specifically about its independence from Holland in 1947 and about the coup of 1965. Indonesia is important not only because it is the land of my national heritage, but because both my parents fought in the revolution of 1947, and because our family was on the short list of people to remove should the Communists have succeeded in 1965. As it was, with the help of family in the military and friends in the Esso Oil Company, my parents, my two sisters, and I fled during the winter of 1965, when General Suharto deposed President Sukarno.

Earlier my younger sister and I had been born in the United States while my dad was studying at Penn State University. He received his PhD in chemical engineering, and we all moved back to Indonesia in 1962. By this time, the Communists had gained a stronger foothold in Indonesian politics. In opposition to Communism, my parents joined the Nationalist Party, which hearkened to the nationalist movement of 1947. They helped start a Nationalist Scouting program, and my dad became the executive officer of the local civil-defense militia. My parents worked to counter not only the influence and effects of Communism but also, and more importantly, to counter the perception that they were no longer good Indonesians because they had been educated in the United States. For my part, Southeast Asia in 1962 was not a pleasant place for an American-born little boy to live. The oral history goes that I fought with just about everybody. Indonesian kids distrusted me because I was American born, while European kids distrusted me because I was Indonesian. I remember a few fights, one in particular—fighting off two boys with a club-sized stick.

While neither of them said as much about their feelings, my parents, I believe, were heartbroken to flee Indonesia, and heartbroken by the political state of the Indonesia they had fought to birth. My biggest clues to this heartbreak were the facts that, first, we didn't speak the Indonesian Bahasa language in our home as we grew up in the United States; and, second, that of our family of five, only my mother had gone back to visit after our return to the United States in 1965. The message of these facts to me was that while I needed to be proud of my Indonesian heritage, I was an American.

I turned eighteen the summer prior to the 1976 presidential elections. In spite of my Republican registration, I was excited about the prospects and possibilities of a "born-again Christian" in the White House. When I factored in the recent Watergate debacle of the Republican Party and the seemingly ineffectual Administration of Gerald Ford, the choice for Jimmy Carter wasn't very difficult. During his administration, however, it didn't seem as if his Christianity made much of an impact on national policy or national politics. It seemed as if his programs had a very difficult time getting through Congress, and it was difficult for me to see how those policies that passed made a real impact on the streets.

By the time the 1980 presidential elections came around, I had become disillusioned with politics as it was defined by the electoral process, and disappointed with Jimmy Carter as a president. I realized that the American political system, by its very design, was bigger than any one president. Even if Jesus Christ himself were president, he would still have to wrestle his programs through a divided Congress. In short, I'm not sure it mattered that Jimmy Carter was a committed, born-again Christian in the White House. I also came to realize that what I was looking for was not a better political party or political system, but rather a Redeemer. True and lasting change for the ills of this country could only happen by the redemptive blood of Jesus. There was not, I concluded, a political system on the face of the earth that could produce true and lasting peace and justice; it was only the broken body and shed blood of Jesus Christ that could produce lasting peace and justice.

Irrelevance: The Kingdom of God
as Non Sequitur to the Nation-State

Steve Long of Garrett-Evangelical Theological Seminary once referred to
Church of the Servant King as irrelevant.[1] This remark was meant as a
compliment, as much as I wish it were true. If we Christians are to find
our primary identity in being the people of God—in a place that is at
the very least called to be ruled by steadfast love, right relationships and
humility (Mic 6.8), then we are, by definition, a political entity. If we, as
the people of God, derive our presuppositions and final ends from the
character of God and the cross of Jesus, then we become irrelevant to the
nation-state.

A central concern of God's people throughout history is their identity. A central theme of Scripture's narrative is an account of Yahweh's
efforts to call and redeem for himself a gathered people on earth to reflect his character. This thread runs consistently from His relationship to
Adam and Eve to his exhortations to the churches in John's Revelation.
To this day, Yahweh continues to want to create a people and place ruled
by the virtues of steadfast love, right relationship and humility (Mic 6:8),
without regard to whatever dominant society in the midst of which the
church finds itself.

This disregard for the dominant society around the church defines
in the first place the inner "life together" of the church. How brothers and
sisters in a local congregation order themselves, how they care for one another, and how they encourage and exhort one another are practices that
find both their presuppositions and final ends in steadfast love, right relationships and humility. Second, how the church relates to the society that
surrounds it (that is to say, the church's "politics") is entirely defined by
being a people and place ruled by steadfast love, right relationships, and
humility. This godly politics is always in tension with and in opposition to
the prevalent system, whether that system is imperialism, Communism,
liberal democracy or another system. Any political system of the world
draws its presuppositions and final ends in coercive power. In contrast,
the New Testament asserts Jesus to be king of the cosmos (Eph 2), and the
glory of his kingship is his servitude to the Father, which leads to the cross
(Phil 2), and never the twain shall meet.

1. Long, "Importance of an Irrelevant Jesus."

Allegiances: The Lordship of Jesus and the Kingdom of God

The proclamation "Jesus is Lord and Savior of my life" is one of those evangelical proclamations that roll off our tongues with nary a thought of what exactly we are saying. We are, in this instance, guilty of the same thoughtless conformity that I accuse my son of as he listens to urban rap music while living in Eugene, Oregon. I believe the word *poseur* is the contemporary label for this sort of thing. To be a poseur is to be disingenuous or even flippant about a subject. For example, my son berates kids who live in the cul-de-sacs of Eugene and who "talk ghetto." A young woman at Theo's Coffee House in Eugene at least feels like a poseur for wearing a Chicago Cubs T-shirt even though she is not really a Cubs fan. And yet the proclamation that "Jesus is Lord" has led and continues to lead our brothers and sisters in the faith to their deaths. Lee Camp of Lipscomb University reminded me that the very phrase "Son of God, Lord and Savior" in reference to Jesus was in the first century an "in-your-face affront" to the Roman Empire.[2] It was a bold declaration by our first-century forebears that it was Jesus who was their Lord, who was their Savior, who was the Son of God, and not Caesar. Somewhere in the world, the proclamation "Jesus is Lord and Savior of my life" has real and significant implications even today. What is the basis of the lordship of Jesus? What is the nature of the kingdom of God? The answer to those questions and our commitment to those answers define our relationship to the nation-state and our participation with the nation-state.

I presuppose a proleptic or overlapping element to the kingdom of God in human history. The kingdom of God, which Jesus ushers in with his life, death, and resurrection, has an element that is here and now, in which we Christians participate. The gospel that Jesus proclaims, which in itself has kingly and political overtones, is that the kingdom of God is at hand, and that the kingdom of God has substantial ramifications for how we relate to one another in the present age, while we yet wait for the kingdom's culmination. We live here and now in the reality that the kingdom of God is also here and now, that the coming age has begun.

> For he is our shalom; in his flesh he has made both groups into one and has broken down the dividing wall, that is, the hostility between us. He has abolished the law with its commandments and

2. Lee Camp visited Church of the Servant King in Eugene, Oregon, on April 28 and 29, 2006.

ordinances, that he might create in himself one new humanity in place of the two, thus making shalom, and might reconcile both groups to God in one body through the cross, thus putting to death that hostility through it. So he came and proclaimed shalom to you who are far off and shalom to you who are near; for through him both of us have access in one Spirit to the Father. So then you are no longer foreigners and aliens, but are citizens with the saints and also members of the household of God. (Eph 2:14–19, author's paraphrase)

The Ephesian epistle is a watershed document for Church of the Servant King. As a manifesto of the kingdom of God, it serves as a template for our aspirations of how life in the kingdom of God should be lived, as well as a declaration of the nature of the kingdom of God and the purposes of Yahweh himself, and how we Christians participate in the kingdom of God. Yahweh has enthroned Jesus and has made him head, far above "all rule and authority and power and dominion . . . in this age and in the age to come" (Eph 1:21, NRSV). The nature of the kingdom of God is nothing short of shalom. Shalom is not the peace in my heart—a peace of which my early evangelical teachers spoke. Neither is shalom merely the absence or cessation of violence, a sort of cosmic détente. Rather, shalom is the presence of right relationships, a unity and reconciliation among brothers and sisters, and between us and the Father. Shalom is the presence of the steadfast love, right relationship, and humility to which the prophet Micah hearkens, as well as the reforging of spears that Isaiah foretells (Isa 2:4).

As brothers and sisters in Christ, we are a new humanity, citizens of heaven, having been called out of our old identities and allegiances. Yahweh calls, adopts, and creates a "citizenry" marked by unity, reconciliation, and shalom. We are no longer Jews or Gentiles, or Greeks or barbarians, or even Indonesian or Pennsylvanian or American. We are Christians, citizens of the kingdom of God; we are the people of God. We are expatriate citizens of the kingdom of God, living in whatever place we happen to find ourselves, whether that place is Eugene, Oregon, or Tokyo, Japan, or Bandung, Indonesia.

Let the same mind be in you as that was in Christ Jesus, who, though he was in the form of God, did not regard equality with God as something to be exploited, but emptied himself, taking the form of a slave, being born of human likeness. And being

found in human form, he humbled himself and became obedient to the point of death—even death on a cross. Therefore God
also highly exalted him and gave him the name that is above every
name, so that at the name of Jesus every knee shall bow in heaven
and on earth and under the earth, and every tongue confess that
Jesus Christ is Lord, to the glory of God the Father. (Phil 2:5–11,
NRSV)

The new humanity ushered in by the life, death, and resurrection
of Jesus is revolutionary and subversive in the extreme. Whereas the Pax
Americana rules by might, the kingdom of God rules by servitude. The
rule of Jesus is not grasped by Jesus in the way that Suharto grasped power
from Sukarno in 1965 Indonesia, nor even in the way George W. Bush
grasped power from Clinton in 2000. By contrast, the rule of Jesus is given
of the Father. Paul is very clear on this point in his Philippian poem, for
which everything comes back to the cross. Yahweh exalts Jesus in direct
response to Jesus's servitude, this emptying of self and humility, leading to
the cross. The New Testament suggests, especially in the gospel accounts
of Jesus's temptation, that he could have grasped at his equal standing
with Yahweh. It is clear by any number of accounts that Jesus chose not to
grasp at his equal standing with Yahweh. Instead Jesus chose to relate to
the Father on the basis of steadfast love, right relationship, and humility.
The exaltation language of the Philippian poem is regal, kingly language.
The Father exalts and bestows. Jesus's name is now above all other names.
Every knee shall bow. Every tongue will confess. Jesus is Lord. Jesus rules
to the glory of God the Father. In every way, Jesus rules the cosmos, and
his rule is absolute. However, Jesus's rule reverses any notion of power
and order, in that Jesus is king precisely because he is servant.

The radical and diametric reversal of power and order brought on
by the rule of Jesus puts the kingdom of God at odds with any and all
power systems of the world. Ultimately, all power systems of the world
find their foundation in the grasping of power. In these systems, the question is always who has hold of the big stick or of the bigger stick. When
all is said and done, every political model is nothing more than a reshuf-
fling of strength and power. The coercive power of foreign imperial rule is
overthrown only to be replaced by the coercive power of the new military
dictatorship. Or the coercive power of a dictator is overthrown only to be
replaced by the coercive power of an occupational force or by the coercive

power of warring factions. Even liberal democracy has its own brand of coercion, falling usually along economic lines.

To all this the kingdom of God runs diametrically opposed. Jesus rules precisely because he humbles himself to the Father. He empties himself, becoming a slave to God. He is obedient to the cross. It is in direct opposition to the established powers that Jesus radicalizes the law in his Sermon on the Mount. He takes conventionally understood law and extends it to radical extremes. Under his rule, it is no longer good enough that I not kill, but I am equally guilty of murder when I am angry. It's no longer good enough that I not sleep with another woman, but I'm equally guilty of adultery when I'm lustful. I am not to resist evil; I am to love my enemies and to pray for those who persecute me. These demands are totally and absolutely incoherent unless I live life from the standpoint of the rule of Jesus as described in Paul's Philippian poem or in the Ephesian epistle.

Regime Change: Lording Over
versus Hope in the Resurrection

In reality, rule on the basis of the grasping of power is incoherent for disciples of Jesus. What is real in light of the life, death, and resurrection of Jesus is that the new age of the kingdom of God has begun here and now. In Jesus, God has broken into human history and established his kingdom, calling for our allegiance to become a new humanity. This new humanity is rooted in nothing less than the cross of Jesus, as its source as well as its very identity. While George W. Bush may claim that the U.S. war on terror is waged to save civilization itself, in reality it is the cross of Jesus that is the true and lasting regime change that will redeem humanity.

Perhaps the pressing question is one of wherein our hope lies. Jacques Ellul speaks of hope addressing the deep need of humanity,[3] and Barry Harvey speaks of hope looking forward to the eschaton and to the resurrection.[4] We Christians live in hope as we declare God's promises. We live in hope by standing fast to those promises. Hope points to what is real in spite of the truth of this or that specific situation. The truth

3. See Ellul, *Hope in Time of Abandonment*.

4. Barry Harvey visited Church of the Servant King in Eugene, Oregon, from April 22 to 24, 2005.

of the world is that we live in a "culture of death," as Pope John Paul II proclaimed.[5] Yet the reality of life is that death has been conquered by the cross of Jesus. Will the ills of society be cured by a different president? Will they be cured by a third party not bought by big-business money? Will they be cured by an altogether different political system or model, be it socialism, Green Party politics, or anarchy? Or will the ills of society be cured by the life, death, and resurrection of Jesus, and by the new age of the kingdom of God inaugurated by Jesus?

For us Christians, the previous sentence ought to be a rhetorical question. But it is not. It never has been and never will be a merely rhetorical question. It is the recurring struggle of God's people not to live as the world lives. Just as the children of Israel in the desert wanted to return to Egypt (Exod 16:3), we in our age constantly want to return to a Christendom married to the powers of the present age. It is so ingrained in us to ask the questions of efficacy and effectiveness: What are the ends? What is effective? What works? In opposition to these questions, the kingdom of God asks questions of faithfulness to the life and call of Jesus. Paul exhorts the church in Rome to be transformed and not conformed (Rom 12:2) precisely because the question of the focus of our hope is never merely rhetorical. We are nonetheless the first fruits of the hope of the new age of the kingdom of God (Rom 8:23–25), and we are called to live in hope.

Perhaps I was fortunate that around the same time when I needed to think through my nationality, wise men of the kingdom who were around me also began asking me questions about Jesus and his lordship. Interwoven in the string of events that I consider to be my conversion experience, which spanned my teen years, were reflections and discussions of whether I should declare myself an American citizen or an Indonesian citizen. The issue of nationality was a central theme as I grew up, not only in the narratives with which I grew up but also in the life of my family. Everything that I heard, and many of the things we did, had nationality as a prominent backdrop. So while there was indeed a spiritual component to my conversion, my decision to be a disciple of Jesus was primarily a decision of nationality and allegiance. The primary question I was answering was, to whom or to what would I pledge my allegiance? What was worth living for and dying for? Who or what indeed reigned supreme?

5. John Paul II, *Evangelium vitae*.

Ultimately no one can claim a specific scriptural injunction to vote or not vote. However, the decision whether or not a Christian should vote is predicated upon our sense of identity and upon the focus of our hope. We Christians have been given a new identity. We are Christians first and foremost, members of the body of Christ, gathered to be the people and place where Jesus is Lord and Savior. The church is that place on earth where life is lived on the basis of the life and call of Jesus—a call to live by steadfast love, right relationships, and humility. This is who we are, and this is our political reality. Will we live trusting in chariots (Isa 31:1), or will we live in the hope of the resurrection of the dead? Will we take Yahweh at his word that death and separation have been conquered by the cross of Jesus, or that the new age of the kingdom of God has dawned here on earth in our time?

We should abstain from voting not out of disdain either for the United States or for any particular candidate or even for the electoral process. We should abstain from voting as a protest, as a testament of our hope in the resurrection of the dead, and of the current presence of the new age of the kingdom of God. In our own historical context, we declare that the kingdom of God is present here and now, and that Jesus Christ is the Son of God, and is our Lord and Savior. George W. Bush is not our lord and savior, the United States of America is not our lord and savior, even liberal democracy is not our lord and savior. This is the reality of human history as it currently stands. In this reality, what happens in Washington DC or Baghdad, Iraq, or Jakarta, Indonesia, is ultimately irrelevant. The rule of Jesus will remain regardless of who wins the 2008 presidential election, or regardless of how the Sunni and Shia factions in Iraq resolve their power struggle. In light of the reality of the age of the kingdom of God, to participate in the processes of the powers of the present age is quite simply incoherent.

9

The "Presidentialdom" of God:
Our Conversation with Pilate

Ted Lewis

Not too long ago I met an elderly Mennonite woman who told me about her father's principled stance for not voting. On occasion he might have voted for candidates on the local scene, but on the whole, he refrained from voting. For him, this was a way of saying that his allegiances were reserved for God alone and could not be shared with a nation-state. In solidarity with her father's leanings, this woman had penciled in "Mickey Mouse" for president in the elections of 2000. As she described this to me, it was quite clear that behind her playful act was a serious attempt to exercise her own liberty of conscience.

I felt a oneness with her perspective on voting. On one hand, both of us shared a sense of the buffoonery of the federal electoral process; that is, of the way that money talks, and of the corporate control of government no matter who is elected. But we also shared a deeper conviction that on the basis of biblical faith, one could have a principled ethic for not voting. Something greater than candidate report cards was at stake for us. The root issue for us was a matter of political identity and allegiance.

Political identity and allegiance. What determines them? What expresses them? We might think of various expressions of patriotism. But being a good citizen, as older generations learned in their high school civics classes, is more than making a good show of it. Good citizenship involves duties. And we fulfill these duties not for our own sake but for the sake of our nation. Voting is certainly one of those duties of good citizenship, but we are also told it is a privilege. Sacrifices were made to create a system in which voting happens; thus voting is a privilege that other countries may not enjoy. Not to vote would be a sign of disregard for the sacrifices that created a land where voting itself can happen. And so one does not easily challenge something bound up with the expression of allegiance to one's nation.

My own voting history falls into four time categories:

1. I voted with personal conviction.

2. I voted without personal conviction.

3. I did not vote, and this action was without personal conviction.

4. I did not vote, and this action was with personal conviction.

Those four periods roughly correspond to the '70s, '80s, '90s, and our current decade. The first period saw my support for Carter, and the last period involved the second Bush administration. I have on occasion voted for third parties, but those choices have had no continuity whatsoever. I have always felt that a candidate's character and track record are to be reckoned with. These factors do count for something, just as they do for church leaders. But what the progression through these stages suggests to me is that a greater set of factors—beyond party platforms, beyond the quality of candidates—brought me to a place of choosing not to vote out of personal conviction. The aim of this essay is to present this greater set of factors.

Overlapping the fourth stage has been my vocational development as a mediator. This work has tuned me into the process side of things, biasing me toward the merits of consensual, "win-win" outcomes. It wasn't until I served on a county-level council with commissioners, mayors, and heads of justice agencies that I fully realized my discomfort with voting. Hand raising and saying aye or nay in a small group carry their own problems; no one likes to stick out. But hand raising aside, I learned that I would prefer to help two parties work together as best they can rather than to throw my lot in with one side.

In this essay I am not going to examine the voting *process*. Other essays could cover the dynamics of majority rule, top-heavy campaign money, and adversarial persuasion techniques. My focus is how the act of voting itself becomes an expression of our political identity not simply in relation to a political party but in relation to our citizenship. How do we demonstrate our political identity? What, in fact, determines our political identity? These are the seminal questions that drove the conversation between Jesus and Pilate, and my hope is that we can draw ourselves into this same conversation.

But first I want to set the stage with some word studies. Origins of the word *vote* go back to the Latin word *votum*, which implies a wish or a prayer. A votive candle is lit, for example, to reinforce one's deepest prayer to a saint or to God. The related words *vow* and *devote* also suggest the personal commitment bound up in the meaning of *votum*. The word *elect* stems back to the Latin *electus*, a form of the root *eligere*, which means "to pick out" or "to choose out." Related here are a set of words: *collect, lecture, lectionary, eligible, diligent* and *neglect*. *Diligent* and *neglect* are tied into a second set of words (*religion, allegiance, oblige, liege*) that all stem from the cousin root *ligare*, which means "to bind" or "to tie." Altogether, the origins of the words *vote* and *elect* appear to emerge from a set of meanings that imply deep loyalty to that which one chooses.

This, then, is my thesis: Voting for political leaders, whether we think about it or not, establishes bonds between people and government in similar ways that religion establishes bonds between people and deities. The question I am raising, therefore, is whether such political bonds are warranted within the context of biblical faith. I will argue that such bonds of allegiance do not fit within the new vision of community set forth in the New Testament. On the positive side, this new vision suggests that our choosing, binding, promising, pledging, and vowing energies are to be expressed for the sake of the *ekklesia*, the "called-out" community, and are not to be expressed for the upbuilding of a state, nation, or empire. Does this assertion imply full disengagement? No. It simply means that expressions of allegiance are reserved for God and for God's elected community, and thus that one's positive engagement in the world will have a new, distinctive look to it.

Emerging out of this shift of loyalty comes a second theme. As our allegiance energies are channeled toward the relational upbuilding of others (that is, as the people of God begin to mirror God's own pattern of sacrificial love), we will then have a greater freedom to leave all outcomes in the hands of God. This does not mean that we have no regard for human agency. All people have the ability to exercise creative gifts and passions. Freely leaving all outcomes in the hands of God does mean, from a faith perspective, that human agency is not the beginning point for whatever ends we may desire. Just as we do not with our hands manufacture deities that help us to harness power for our own interests, so we do not with our hands manufacture political efforts that help us to secure power for our particular interest group. The same principle could be applied to taking vengeance into our own hands. In brief, leaving outcomes to God means that we are invited to refrain from certain political investments to the extent that they either require no genuine trust in God or reveal any aspect of God's character. Conversely, our political engagements will be distinguished by our trust in God and by our bearing witness to God's truth, both within the church and toward the world through the church.

Jesus's Conversation with Pilate

N. T. Wright once suggested that what Jesus was to the people of Israel, the church is to be to the world. The body of Christ is meant to carry on the work that Jesus inaugurated. Jesus set the mold for engaging the limited world of his day, and if the church finds a different mold, then it is working off a different gospel. And so as I begin to look into some biblical texts, I want to be open about my assumption that the church community is continually invited to take its cues from the way Jesus understood and carried out his mission.

It didn't take long for Jesus to hit this missional bull's-eye in his dialogue with Pilate (John 18). "For this I was born, and for this I came into the world, to testify to the truth" (v. 18). "To testify," "to bear witness": the Greek word is *martureō*, from which we get our word *martyr*. But the primary usage of *martureō* is simply "to reveal something," just as witnesses to a crime would testify to the truth of what they saw. Jesus continues, "Everyone who belongs to the truth listens to my voice" (v. 37). This is quite a politically saturated statement. Followers are implied. There is a leader with a commanding voice. Personal commitment is suggested. All of this stirs Pilate's imagination with respect to Jesus's own view of truth.

"What is truth?" (v. 38). Pilate has the last word in this conversation. The Gospel writer allows the question to steep within his readers. But what drives Pilate's inquiry? Was he interested in a full-bodied answer? No. If he had been, more dialogue likely would have followed, as dialogue followed with Nicodemus in John 3. On the other hand, was Pilate making a sharp, cynical reply? As a relativist or materialist, skeptical of the validity of all metaphysical truth, does he give a short, breathy laugh before asking his question? Again, I'd say no. The text offers no clues to reinforce this angle.

Pilate's question is neither philosophical nor cynical. It is simply the response of a seasoned politician. And Jesus has nothing more to say to a politician, reasonable as Pilate may be. Pilate is a political realist. He comes across as a moderate governor who prides himself in making sound, civil judgments for the good of society. He has to deal with extremisms of all sorts on a weekly (if not daily) basis. Over time, he's gotten good at it. He can smell out false charges and deliver good justice for the accused. Luke's account of Pilate actually has him going out of his way in five statements to protect Jesus from the ill intents of the Jewish leaders: "I have found . . . no basis for your charges against him . . . As you can see, he has done nothing to deserve death" (Luke 23:14–15).

Pilate is a fair, law-abiding politician. Yet he is also a shrewd, utilitarian politician. He does not want extremism ever to get the upper hand. He understands the need for compromises. He can befriend Herod in a single day if he chooses; he can have someone flogged and call it good; he can be part of deals and bargains. In the end, he can give in to a majority vote and wash his hands of personal responsibility. Pilate understands the power he holds, and for the most part, that is all the truth he knows and needs to know. It is in this context that he asks, "What is truth?" In other words, "What does any nonpolitical or metaphysical truth have to do with the real world in which I operate?"

The interpretive keys, therefore, that unlock John 18 are primarily those phrases with political content. Of these phrases, the most important ones involve kingship. All four Gospel accounts have Pilate asking Jesus, "Are you the king of the Jews?" Behind this inquiry are deeper questions: "What sort of king are you, anyway? Are you some sort of a rebel leader?"

Jesus probes a bit to find out how Pilate came up with this king-of-the-Jews reference. "Is that your own idea, or did you hear about me from others?" (v. 34). Jesus is perhaps testing Pilate's awareness of messianic kingship within the Jewish context.

"Look here," says Pilate. "I hardly know anything about messianic kings. I'm not a Jew. What's funny about this situation is that it's your own people who are turning you in. You must have done something really bad that they cannot accept. What did you do? If it is not criminal, my guess is that I can get you off the hook" (v. 35).

Jesus does not want to go down the path of explaining what he has done. He has no inclination to defend himself. The real issue is not his actions but his foundations. It is precisely at this point in the dialogue that he realizes his moment to delineate his political identity from a conventional approach. Note that in this move he refrains from the typical manner of using political or historical truth to defend one's cause. Jesus does not defend his own integrity:

"I operate in a kingdom that is very different from normal kingdoms in this world. If it were similar, my followers would take up arms to prevent me from being handed over to the Jews. They would fight on behalf of me and my cause. But being under the power of the Jewish leaders poses no problem to the nature of my kingdom. That's because this kingdom has nothing in common with the way power is normally leveraged."

"Ah, you really are a king, then. You used the phrase 'my kingdom'" (v. 37). Pilate is proud of himself for finding a way to keep his hands tight on the reins of the conversation. All this talk of "normal" and "different from normal" is talk he would rather sidestep.

"In a certain respect you are right. I am a king. I have followers. I have been a leader. But true power comes in the relinquishment of ego power, ethnic power, and worldly power. Actually, the main purpose for my whole existence here on earth is to simply bear witness to God's truth. Everyone who resonates with this truth and also reveals it in their own lives is part of my kingdom" (v. 37).

"What is truth?" (v. 38).

Either Jesus remains silent, as the other Gospel accounts emphasize, or Pilate uses the question to state that he has had the last word in the conversation. As readers, we sense that the conversation is half baked; perhaps Pilate, like most of us, does not want to be confronted with the full implications of Jesus's view of things for his own life. At any rate, Pilate has work to do. The extremists are yelling in front of the palace, and the day is getting on. He has heard enough of Jesus to know that Jesus is not a serious threat to the Pax Romana—certainly not as threatening as an insurrectionist leader like Barabbas. "Thank goodness," Pilate thinks to himself, "that the rebel, Barabbas, was recently captured. He most certainly will be brought to justice." And with these thoughts, Pilate steps out before the restless crowd.

"Do you want me to release 'the King of the Jews'?" he shouts (v. 39).

Political by Default

If *politics* can loosely be defined as the management of power in social relations, and if Jesus rejected participation in the normal politics of his day, then it is understandable how Jesus's new orientation, powerful as it was in its influence, was politically charged. By offsetting conventional ways of maneuvering power, such as fighting, resisting, defending, paying, appeasing, lobbying, and so forth, Jesus's new way became political by default.

The assumption I am now making is that if voting had been part of the conventional landscape of his day, Jesus and his followers would have not participated in it. The politics of Jesus began with the rejection of conventional power and proceeded with the positive activity of bearing witness to God's core qualities: sacrificial love, covenantal faithfulness, and reconciling justice. The Sanhedrin already knew that this Galilean's approach was political, because it disturbed the status quo. Many Jewish leaders perceived the threat all along. And because the message and way of Jesus had powerful influence (and thus competed on the political landscape), the termination of Jesus seemed the only solution.

In this setting, Jesus aligned himself not only with the Israelite prophetic tradition but also with the Israelite kingly tradition. Yet there were ambiguities to his kingly identity that Jesus seemed to accept. From the donkey ride on Palm Sunday to his teaching on the Davidic psalm (Psalm 110) to the wearing the purple robe and thorny crown, the passion narratives present Jesus as a messianic king. Even Pilate wanted this advertised on the cross. But what an unusual king! We as readers are often uneasy with the weakness and humiliation running through these royal images. Little wonder that most first-century Jews were not prepared for a messiah who would be more lamblike than lionlike. In a jolting way, the very paradigm of kingship was turned upside down, and like many people in first-century Palestine, most Christians today are hesitant to give up their King-David imagery for making sense of God's rule.

What we cannot overlook is the contents of this upside-down kingship, contents that correlate with God's core attributes. If Jesus had made a fuller reply to Pilate's final question, the language of his reply may have echoed the Prologue to John's Gospel. Truth was not in reference to historical or philosophical or even doctrinal matters. We are dealing with truth in the Hebrew sense, where the word *truth* is inseparable from "faithfulness" or "trustworthiness." We are talking about God's being true as a yardstick is true, or as drums and discs of a car's brakes are true. The second cardinal character trait for God in the Hebrew Scriptures was steadfast love or mercy, and thus we recognize the duet in the phrase from John's Prologue: "full of grace and truth" (John 1:14). This recognition of the way God's core relational qualities were revealed in Jesus led to a radical reformulation of the older concept of God's glory.

No wonder that John used the metaphor of light to complement this matrix of divine qualities. As Jesus revealed divine truth (in successive "signs" throughout John's Gospel) by showing unconditional love among people who had less power, less status, and less belonging, Jesus exposed the inner contradictions of a society that masked all disparities. Normal politics prefers a seamless unity whereby God and nationalism, faith and wealth, security and military power dovetail. Even incongruent ends and means can blend together. The stakes are higher in Jesus's own day because the Pax Romana resists any disturbance, and the Jewish institutions survive within a delicate balance between Roman power and restless people-power. It is in this context that Jesus's new way is a political threat, because love, grace, justice, and fidelity, when put into practice, truly upset this tense social order. Given the social influence of the new way, Jesus does not avoid a kingly identity.

The word king in Old English is allied to our words kin and kind. A king led a tribe of people bound by kinship ties. Jesus affirms this ancient meaning when he tells Pilate that his followers will know his voice, and that this voice is in unity with Jesus's vocation to testify to the truth. Since it is no longer by blood lines but by participatory belief that followers are bound to their new leader, their involvement in the new kingdom will be marked by demonstrations of God's truth, and again, the content of this truth, when enacted, puts them at odds with conventional structures of power.

The new kingdom is manifested within the new kinship group. As Jesus is viewed as the head of this new body of people, he becomes the unifying point for the diversity of members. Such unity, as the New Testament suggests, is based on the vision of members participating in the pattern of their leader, "follow[ing] in his steps" (1 Pet 2:21). The new community, therefore, becomes a political entity by default in the midst of other political institutions *precisely at the point that it embodies these new practices*. Again, the new community becomes a political body not only because the new way invites refraining from certain political practices, but, more so, because the new way invites the proactive commitment to show *agape* love in all relationships. At its root, the New Testament bids us to invest our social and political energies in new ways and in new places: in relationships that are undervalued, in reconciliation processes, in healing ministries, in sharing economic goods. "Bearing witness to the truth" becomes the missional motto for the church, and the type of trust required to do such work is a trust that leaves all outcomes in the hands of God.

The "Presidentialdom" of God

Allow me to contemporize Jesus's language in his conversation with Pilate:

"My presidentialdom is not of a governmental nature. If it were, my followers would certainly be lobbying and voting for me to advance my cause. But my presidentialdom is of a completely different nature that involves other activity."

"Ah, so you are a president, then. A CEO, perhaps."

"In a manner of speaking, you could say that. But not as you would think of a president or CEO. My main calling in life is to reveal God's truth, not to advance my own leadership or to do whatever it takes to reach certain ends. And those who fall under my company equally aim to reveal this truth, leaving all outcomes to God rather than trying to make things happen strictly by their own efforts."

"What's truth got to do with being a president?"

Jesus has nothing more to say. He already hit the bull's-eye of what he wanted to say. And the asker has nothing more to ask. The asker has come to an uneasy awareness that the two orientations, while having common language, have little else in common.

You may think this is a big leap to go from kingdom to presidentialdom. But let me suggest a midway option: "Caesardom." Certainly Rome didn't have a democratic electoral process, but it was nonetheless a civil, respectable system of government involving a senate and courts. An interesting question might be, if among Roman citizens voting had been part of the framework, and if you had been a Roman Christian, would you have voted for a Caesar (given a situation of choosing between two or more candidates)? In a more poignant way, the issue of allegiance comes up strongly since the deification of Caesars was mingled with expressions of loyalty.

At some level, the Philippians had to wrestle with such issues. Philippi was a an important Roman colony, and the church there included a good part of Roman citizens who were also Jews. Twice Paul employs the word *politeuma* to show that the "citizenship" of the Philippian church members has a new, distinctive claim over them (1:27; 3:20). In a sense, Paul is saying, "Your political energies are now to be rechanneled into your relational activity as a new community." The church, then, becomes a new *polis* (city). In both Philippians 1:27 and Philippians 3:20, Paul focuses on conduct. In the first reference, the phrase that includes *politeuma* is best translated, "conduct your *citizenship*," but most versions simply have, "live your life." But there's more to it. One's political conduct should be done in "a manner worthy of the gospel of Christ." What does this new conduct look like when one's citizenship has shifted from Rome to kingdom of God?

This tension between Rome and the kingdom of God gets played out in the famous theological hymn of chapter 2. Jesus empties himself not of God's core relational qualities (for Jesus's mission was to reveal these godly traits) but of a supposed sense of self-importance that would be fitting for a Greek or Roman deity during Jesus's era. Jesus cast off the self-important form of Godness and took on a new form of Godness that resembled a slave. His voluntary descent took him as far away from the status of a deified Caesar than anyone in the Mediterranean world could imagine. And in circumstances far worse than those a servant or slave would face, Jesus was executed on a Roman cross. But God exalted him for the divine, redemptive mission of revealing the core qualities of God's Godness, namely, sacrificial love and humility. Such vindication was a major slap in the face of not only Roman politics but the Roman cultural framework of honor and glory. The result of this grand reversal is that even caesars will have to bend the knee to this Lord of *all* rulers.

It is less known that the context of Philippians 2:5–11 is Paul's appeal for relational unity. By individuals considering the interests of others to be more important than any one individual's interests, the practices of humility and love distinguish the new community. Such sharing in the pattern of Jesus will result in tensions and conflicts with Roman society, and likely with institutional aspects of Jewish society. This participation, this sharing, this *koinonia* (a word frequently used in Philippians) involves two spiritual postures: accepting the way of the cross and expecting the way of resurrection. The first is our work: being obedient to God's way and will, and thereafter bearing the consequences. The second is God's work: bringing new life out of hardship, sacrifice and death. What combines the two postures is our trust. We do the work of loving and serving others, knowing that as we do this work, we are shining the spotlight on the One who is Love. At the same time, we leave the outcomes in the hands of God because we are not invested in activities that secure the fulfillment of our own interests.

As God in Christ has taken a reversed orientation to kingship, refusing to employ the usual methods of power and deception and self-promotion, so we are asked to enter into this same pattern, if indeed we are *akin* to him. As we rub against the conventional presidentialdoms of our day, our reversed orientation leads us to not partake fully in the normal patterns of today's politics; this nonparticipation, in my estimation, includes refraining from voting, just as nonparticipation would also include a refraining from pledging allegiance to a nation.

The Means and the Ends

To come full circle with Jesus and Pilate, we recall that Jesus is not defensive. He is not reaching for any means within his disposal to ensure a specific outcome for his cause. Peter later recognizes that this nondefensiveness is most evident in his speech during his passion trials, when he chose not to fight fire with fire: "no deceit was found in his mouth, . . . when reviled he did not retaliate, but rather entrusted himself to the one who judges justly" (1 Pet 2:22–23, NIV). This nondefensiveness is presented as an example for us to follow. Throughout Peter's first letter, readers are invited to conduct their lives with integrity, and if this conduct leads to disempowerment, Peter encourages the faithful to accept these social consequences, hard as they may be. Here we see in broad daylight the call for trust that leaves the outcomes in the hands of God.

We have now come to a deeper consideration of the relation between means and ends. First is the matter of congruence or incongruence. In normal politics, means are subservient to ends. From a publicity standpoint, means and ends do not have to be integrally related. Because the achievements of party interests and national interests are held so high, the justification of any means to reach necessary ends is itself part of the political process. Such justifications can always make people or policies look better than they really are. From God's perspective, however, means and ends always have an integral relationship, and if the means are stained by degrees of corruption or self-interest, then the ends will inevitably be colored by these stains.

Within the kingdom or "presidentialdom" of God, there is always integrity between means and ends. A good tree bears good fruit. In this way, God's mode of reconciling humanity to himself is congruent with the outcome of reconciliation on all levels. Sacrificial peacemaking for the sake of others reflects the very character of God, and this character is the very image into which humanity is gradually being transformed. Just as it can be said that God's future entered into the present when Jesus inaugurated the new kingdom, so it can be said that Jesus embodies God's end in our midst. But Jesus is more than a preview of the end; he is both trail and trailblazer that gets us to the end, and in this sense Jesus is the means of God at work on our behalf.

For Christians, this has huge implications. It means that we no longer need to worry about outcomes. It means we no longer need to take things into our own hands and make things happen a certain way. It means that security issues are redefined for us. We do not need to invest heavily in protecting ourselves. It means we do not have to interfere with the natural unfolding of events, even when events bring plenty of hardships. On the positive side, our putting the outcomes of life in God's hands means that we can concentrate on the integrity of our means, that is, on our conduct, knowing that it is enough to simply make sure our efforts are congruent with the ends of God revealed in the life and work of Jesus. That Jesus is the means and ends of God means that our social and political energies can be invested in *agape* love since we know that sacrificial love is at once the ultimate means in concert with the ultimate ends. By this and by this alone will others know that we are identified with a new messiah (John 13:35).

But, it could be asked, what do Christians do in the face of great evil and corruption? Not interfere? Offer no protection? Simply have radical trust that things will iron themselves out? If we follow the model of Jesus, we will definitely have a model of engagement as opposed to nonengagement. The key is that in the face of evil, neither are we overcome by evil (by, say, absorbing it into our fears and worries), nor are we left with the sole option of fighting against evil on its own terms of force. Instead we engagingly overcome evil with good. True trust in the God of all ends prompts us to bring the best of God's means into the very arena. In the pattern of Jesus, we are asked to bring love, truth, integrity of conduct (indeed any form of good) to bear upon the darkness at hand. Specifically, this call of Jesus means that we will value relationships in our peacemaking activities.

Out of this relational ethic flows the second aspect to the means-and-ends issue, namely, the matter of heavy-handedness versus yieldedness. Participants in the realm of conventional politics are heavily invested in obtaining certain ends, and thus they heavily invest in certain means. Congruence is not at stake; expedience rules the day. If conventional politics all runs in the same direction as idolatry, and the preoccupation with certain ends joins a preoccupation with orchestrating the necessary means to achieve maximum protection or provision from the gods. The result is that our participation shapes our very being—our identity: "Those who trust in [idols] will become like them" (Ps 115:8). I contend that in our national context, the act of voting leads to a similar participation, which subtly distances us from a truer participation in God's vision for a distinguished, "called-out" people. One distinguishing mark of this new people is the quality of yieldedness when social, political, relational engagements are concerned. Again, though, yieldedness is not passivity or withdrawal. Sacrificial love has its own forceful influence.

Voting and Two Masters

I am not suggesting to refrain from voting based on candidate profiles or based on the nature of the electoral process. I am suggesting that the very act of voting itself is problematic in the same way that participating in warfare or in retributive punishments would be problematic for Christians. Below the surface, voting implies a *devotedness* that cannot mix the politics of this world with the politics of Jesus. Just as Jesus's maxim about mammon (Matt 6:24, Luke 16:13) states that we cannot serve two masters, so in matters of politics we cannot serve two masters at once. The real question is, how is our political identity revealed to others? Do we want our political identity to be in conformity with national expectations, or do we want our political identity to be known for its association with a unique, living God?

In the end, choosing not to vote becomes a confession of faith: we are proclaiming our bond to a different master (to a different king, lord, ruler, or president). We come to confess: "Life is not about us and our interests. It's not about our thinking that we can make a difference. Life is about something bigger. It's about God's drama in which we are invited to participate." In this light, indifference about or frustration with politics are never adequate foundations for not voting. Our choice not to vote should always be driven by our deeper motivation to bear witness to the truth. The same motivation steers Christian pacifism. Christian nonparticipation is not simply a matter of refraining from an act, so that nonparticipation itself becomes the final mark. With simple nonparticipation as the goal of Christian action, self-righteousness sets in. Rather, Christian nonparticipation is a matter of living a higher calling, whereby our whole life—our whole conduct—is congruent with the peacemaking ways of God.

The most important question for the faith-based, principled nonvoter is, where do I now invest the political energy that I did not spend through voting? It is the proactive place of new investment that becomes the strongest way to testify to the truth; the new investment of energy serves to place one's identity around positive activity and not just around refraining from activity. As Paul would possibly have said, If I refrain from voting and refrain from participating in war, but have not love, all my nonparticipation amounts to nothing. Where, then, do we channel our love? We channel a large portion into our church communities for the sake of building one another up and modeling a healthy, reconciled community to the world. And we channel a large portion of outward to society. We are to channel our love outward from the center of our church experience (and not as an independent activity, good as such an independent effort may be), for the sake of sharing our blessing, as God would have it to be shared.

Precisely because we choose not to vote *out of conviction*, we heighten our engagement with the broader society. Our choosing not to vote thus raises us out of the mire of political apathy or cynicism. We rise with desires to bear witness to God, to show our new loyalties. Again, our active refraining leads to proactive engagement. Our rejection of normal power management opens up new spaces for us to express God's unique way of dealing with people and power, both within the church and beyond the church. But there's a further level of engagement to which some, but not all, are called. Certain people of faith have special callings to interact with institutions of power. This interaction might involve justice work, advocacy, diplomacy, relief work, and so forth. Among prophetic works, there is a continuum of insiders and outsiders, from Isaiah's advising kings in Jerusalem to Ezekiel's doing artistic acts in a foreign land. Whether service-based or prophetic, significant engagement bears some sort of witness to God's truth, that is, to God's character.

Inevitably, the choice not to vote can become a recognized ecclesial practice. Members of a church can collectively confess their political and covenantal allegiances for God and one another, asserting that their loyalties cannot be divided between two masters. This political and covenantal language fits with the language of how God "has made us to be a kingdom" (Rev 1:6), a unique presidentialdom with a different mode of operation from normal presidentialdoms. Yet the formation of God's community, which is the central concern of the entire Bible, never justifies indifference to the rest of the world or to creation. There is a bigger end at stake in which "all things" are reconciled together. The church, then, never exists for itself. It stands in the trajectory of God's promise to Abraham, whereby the blessing of God's called-out people extends to "all peoples on earth" (Gen 12:3, NIV).

We close, then, imagining ourselves in conversation with Pilate, with one who only understands politics from the point of view of human agency and expedience. He can get us off the hook. We can defend our positions and interests, and perhaps go back to Galilee. Or, if we choose, we can steer the conversation by saying that we operate out of a completely different political context, one that prizes divine revelation and human relationality. The risk of taking this position, though, is that as we claim an alternative political identity, we may suffer consequences that involve shame and disgrace. At a minimum, we will be misunderstood by the majority. In the end, if we have the courage to testify to God's newness through this nonaction, it will be our belief in the power of *agape* love that leads us to refrain from participating in the conventional forms of power management. This trust in the power of *agape* love would, to be sure, reflect the nature of our true citizenship.

Bibliography

Alexander, Paul. "Spirit Empowered Peacemaking: Toward a Pentecostal Charismatic Peace Fellowship." *Journal of the European Pentecostal Theological Association* 22 (2002) 78–102.

Allen, John L. Jr. "As Vatican Calls for Peace, Diplomat Plans Defense of 'Preventive War.'" *National Catholic Reporter*, January 31, 2003. Accessed February 4, 2008. Online: http://ncronline.org/NCR_Online/archives/013103/013103j.htm.

Associated Press, "Legislative Pay Raise before Pennsylvania Top Court." *Lancaster New Era*, April 4, 2006.

Aquinas, Thomas. *Summa Theologica*. Translated by Fathers of the English Dominican Province. 5 vols. Westminster, MD: Christian Classics, 1981.

Baker, James A. III., et al. *The Iraq Study Group Report*. New York: Vintage, 2006.

Barth, Karl. *Church and State*. Church Classics. Translated by G. Ronald Howe. Greenville, SC: Smyth & Helwys, 1991.

———. *Church Dogmatics. The Doctrine of Reconciliation*. Vol. 4. Translated by Geoffrey W. Bromiley. Edited by G. W. Bromiley and T. F. Torrance. Edinburgh, NY, and London: T. & T. Clark, 1958–2004.

———. *Church Dogmatics*. Vol. 4, part 1, *The Doctrine of Reconciliation*. Translated by G. W. Bromiley. Edited by G. W. Bromiley and T. F. Torrance. New York: Scribners, 1956.

———. *Offene Briefe 1935–1942*. Edited by Dieter Koch. Zürich: Theologischer, 2001.

———. *Offene Briefe 1945–1968*. Edited by Dieter Koch. Zürich: Theologischer, 1984.

Bartleman, Frank. "The European War," *The Weekly Evangel*, July 10, 1915.

———. "What Will the Harvest Be?" *The Weekly Evangel*, August 7, 1915.

Bergner, Daniel. "The Other Army." *The New York Times Magazine*, August 14, 2005, 29–35.

Billingsley, Andrew. *Mighty Like a River: The Black Church and Social Reform*, New York: Oxford University Press, 1999.

Bourrie, Mark. "Group Has One Way to Stomach the Choices." *Toronto Star*, November 21, 2000.

Boyer, Peter J. "The Right to Choose: Why the Democrats are Moving Toward Compromise." *New Yorker*, November 14, 2005, 52–61.

Brunelli, Lucio. "No to 'Preventive War.'" Accessed January 26, 2008. Online: http://www.catholicpeacefellowship.org/nextpage.asp?m=2246.

Cahill, Lisa Sowle. *Love Your Enemies: Discipleship, Pacifism, and Just War Theory*. Minneapolis: Fortress, 1994.

CanWest News Service. "Ballot Is No Snack." *Montreal Gazette*, January. 20, 2006.

Cavanaugh, William T. "Killing for the Telephone Company: Why the Nation-State Is Not the Keeper of the Common Good." *Modern Theology* 20 (2004) 243–74.

————. *Theopolitical Imagination: Discovering the Liturgy as a Political Act in an Age of Globalization.* London: T. & T. Clark, 2002.

Christian, Spencer, and Tom Biracree. *Electing Our Government: Everything You Need to Know to Make Your Vote Really Count.* New York: St. Martin's Griffin, 1996.

Cuomo, Mario. "Religious Belief and Public Morality: A Catholic Governor's Perspective." September 13, 1984. University of Notre Dame, Notre Dame, IN. No pages. Accessed February 4, 2008. Online: http://pewforum.org/docs/index.php?DocID=14.

DeNavas-Walt, Carmen, et al. *Income, Poverty, and Health Insurance Coverage in the United States.* Current Population Reports: Consumer Income P60. Washington DC: Bureau of the Census, 2003.

Dictionary.com Unabridged, *version 1.0.1.* Accessed October 1, 2006 http://dictionary.reference.com/search?q=vote.

Drew, Christopher. "U.S. Bars Lab From Testing Electronic Voting." *New York Times*, January 4, 2007.

Dubner, Stephen J., and Steven D. Levitt. "Why Vote?" *The New York Times Sunday Magazine*, November 6, 2005.

Dyck, Cornelius J., and Dennis D. Martin, editors. *The Mennonite Encyclopedia: A Comprehensive Reference Work on the Anabaptist-Mennonite Movement.* 5 vols. Hillsboro, KS: Mennonite Brethren, 1955–1990.

Eller, Vernard. *Christian Anarchy: Jesus' Primacy over the Powers.* Grand Rapids: Eerdmans, 1987.

Ellul, Jacques. *Hope in Time of Abandonment.* Translated by C. Edward Hopkin. New York: Seabury, 1973.

————. *Reason for Being: A Meditation on Ecclesiastes.* Translated by Geoffrey W. Bromiley. Grand Rapids: Eerdmans. 1990.

Ertman, Thomas. *Birth of the Leviathan: Building States and Regimes in Medieval and Early Modern Europe.* Cambridge: Cambridge University Press, 1997.

Fisher, Jonathan. "Kerry Says He Believes Life Starts at Conception." *Washington Post*, July 5, 2004, A6. Accessed January 26, 2008. Online: http://www.washingtonpost.com/ac2/wp-dyn/A27920-2004Jul4?language=printer.

Frazier, Edward Franklin. *The Negro Church in America.* New York: Schocken, 1964.

Frodsham, Stanley H. "Our Heavenly Citizenship," *The Weekly Evangel*, September 11, 1915.

Galloway, Joseph L. "Bush Is Still Not Ready to Listen to Dissenters." *Charleston Gazette*, December 17, 2006.

Giddens, Anthony. *The Nation-State and Violence.* Berkeley: University of California Press, 1987.

Ginsberg, Benjamin. *The Consequences of Consent: Elections, Citizen Control, and Popular Acquiescence.* Reading, MA: Addison-Wesley, 1982.

Grant, George. *English-Speaking Justice.* Toronto: House of Anansi, 1985.

Green Party of the United States. "Cobb Calls for Voting Rights and Reform." No pages. Accessed February 5, 2008. Online: http://www.gp.org/press/pr_07_20_04.html.

Hamilton, John. *Voting in an Election.* Edina, MN: ABDO, 2005.

Hartzler, Lloyd. *The Christian and the State.* Harrisonburg: Christian Light, 1993.

Hauerwas, Stanely. "Democratic Time: Lessons Learned from Yoder and Wolin." *Crosscurrents* 55 (2006) 534–52.

Hertzberg, Hendrik. "Count 'Em," *New Yorker*, March 6, 2006, 27–28.

Hill, Steven. *Fixing Elections: The Failure of America's Winner Take All Politics.* New York: Routledge, 2002.

Hilsenrath, Jon E., and Sholnn Freeman. "The Two-Track Economy: The Rich Get a Leg Up, the Poor Feel the Crunch." *Wall Street Journal,* classroom edition, October 2004. No pages. Accessed February 5, 2008. Online: http://wsjclassroomedition.com/ archive/04oct/econ_recovery.htm.

Horst, Amos S. *The Christian Nonresistant Way of Life.* 4th ed. Ephrata, PA: Weaverland Conference Mennonites, 1998. Originally published 1940 by Peace Problems Committee and Tract Editors of Lancaster Conference District.

Horst, Paul. "Nonresistance and Nonparticipation in Civil Government." Crockett, Kentucky: Rod and Staff n.d. Accessed February 1, 2006. Online: http://www .anabaptists.org/ras/21e74.html.

Human Rights Watch. "Punishment and Prejudice: Racial Disparities in the War on Drugs." Vol. 12, No. 2, May 2000. Accessed December 10, 2006. Online: http://www. hrw.org/reports/2000/usa/Rcedrg00-01.htm.

John XXIII. *Pacem in Terris: Peace on Earth.* In *Catholic Social Thought: The Documentary Heritage,* edited by David J. O'Brien and Thomas A. Shannon, 129–62. Maryknoll, NY: Orbis, 1992.

"John Kerry on Faith." Accessed February 5, 2008. Online: http://www.beliefnet.com/ story/149/story_14928_1.html.

John Paul II. "Address to the Diplomatic Corps." Speech delivered on January 13, 2003. Accessed February 4, 2008. Online: http://www.vatican.va/holy_father/john _paul_ii/speeches/2003/january/documents/hf_jp-ii_spe_20030113_diplomatic -corps_en.html.

———. *Evangelium Vitae.* Accessed n.d. Online: http://www.vatican.va/holy_father/ john_paul_ii/encyclicals/documents/hf_jp-ii_enc_25031995_evangelium-vitae _en.html.

———. "No Peace without Justice, No Justice without Forgiveness." Message delivered for the World Day of Peace, January 1, 2002. Accessed January 26, 2008. Online: http://www.vatican.va/holy_father/john_paul_ii/messages/peace/documents/hf_jp-ii_mes_20011211_xxxv-world-day-for-peace_en.html.

———. *Sollicitudo Rei Socialis: On Social Concern.* In *Catholic Social Thought: The Documentary Heritage,* edited by David J. O'Brien and Thomas A. Shannon, 393–436. Maryknoll, NY: Orbis, 1992.

Kauffman, Daniel, editor. *Doctrines of the Bible.* Scottdale, PA: Mennonite, 1928.

Keyssar, Alexander. "The Right to Vote and Election 2000." In *The Unfinished Election of 2000,* edited by Jack N. Rakove, 75–102. New York: Basic, 2001.

King, Martin Luther, Jr. *Why We Can't Wait.* A Mentor Book. New York: New American Library, 1964.

Kornweibel, Theodore, Jr., "Race and Conscientious Objection in World War I: The Story of the Church of God in Christ." In *Proclaim Peace: Christian Pacifism from Unexpected Quarters,* edited by Theron Schlabach and Richard Hughes, 58–81. Urbana: University of Illinois Press, 1997.

Kuhn, David Paul. "Kerry's Top Ten Flip-Flops." *CBS Evening News,* broadcast September 29, 2004. Accessed February 4, 2008. Online: http://www.cbsnews.com/ stories/2004/09/29/politics/printable646435.shtml

Lampman, Jane. "A Crusade After All? " *Christian Science Monitor*, April 17, 2003. Accessed January 26, 2008. Online: //www.commondreams.org/headlines03/0417-03.htm

Lawrence, Jill. "'Intelligent design' backers lose in Pennsylvania." *USA Today*, November 9, 2005. Accessed February 4, 2008. Online: http://www.usatoday.com/news/education/2005-11-09-pennsylvania-intelligent-design_x.htm

Lay Commission on Catholic Social Teaching and the U.S. Economy. *Toward the Future: Catholic Social Thought and the U.S. Economy: A Lay Letter.* New York: Lay Commission on Catholic Social Teaching and the U.S. Economy, 1984.

Lehman, Chester K. "The Christian and Civil Government." In *Bible Teaching on Nonconformity*, 39–44. Publishing Committee of the Mennonite Publications Board. Scottdale, PA: Mennonite Publishing House, 1940. Reprinted, Ephrata, PA: Weaverland, 1998.

Lincoln, C. Eric. *The Black Church Since Frazier.* Sourcebooks in Negro History. New York: Schocken, 1974.

Lincoln, C. Eric, and Lawrence H. Mamiya, *The Black Church in the African-American Experience.* Durham: Duke University Press, 1990.

Lindsay, A. D. *The Essentials of Democracy.* 2d edition. William J. Cooper Foundation Lectures, Swarthmore College, 1929. Oxford: Clarendon, 1967.

———. *The Modern Democratic State.* New York: Oxford University Press, 1943.

Long, D. Stephen. "The Importance of an Irrelevant Jesus: The Subversive Nature of Traditional Christian Doctrine." Church and Culture Lecture, Eugene, OR, February 7–9, 2003.

MacIntyre, Alisdair C. *Dependent Rational Animals: Why Human Beings Need the Virtues.* Paul Carus Lecture Series 20. Chicago: Open Court, 1999.

Maestro, Betsy. *The Voice of the People.* Illustrated by Giulio Maestro. New York: Lothrop, Lee & Shepard, 1996.

Manent, Pierre. *An Intellectual History of Liberalism.* Translated by Rebecca Balinksi, with a foreword by Jerrold Seigel. New French Thought. Princeton: Princeton University Press, 1994.

Mann, Thomas E. "Redistricting Reform." *National Voter*, June 2005, 4–6. Accessed February 1, 2006. Online: http://www.lwv.org

Martin, Isaac D. *The Christian and the World.* Crockett, KY: Rod and Staff, 2001.

McCafferty, William Burton. "Should Christians Go To War?" *The Christian Evangel*, January 16, 1915.

Moore, Stanley W., James Lare, and Kenneth A. Wagner. *The Child's Political World: A Longitudinal Perspective.* New York: Praeger, 1985.

National Association of Independent Colleges and Universities. *Your Vote—Your Voice.* Accessed December 2006. Online: http://www.naicu.edu/docLib/20070312_YourVoteYourVoice_2006.pdf.

Norman, Martha Prescodd. "Shining in the Dark: Black Women and the Struggle for the Vote, 1955–1965." In *African American Women and the Vote, 1837–1965*, edited by Ann D. Gordon, et al., 172–99. Amherst: University of Massachusetts Press, 1997.

Novak, Michael. "An Argument That War against Iraq Is Just." *Origins* 32 (2003) 593, 596.

———. *The Catholic Ethic and the Spirit of Capitalism.* New York: Free Press, 1993.

Null, David. *An Introduction to Mennonite Doctrine and Practice.* Crockett, KY: Rod and Staff, 2004.

O'Brien, David J., and Thomas A. Shannon, editors, *Catholic Social Thought: The Documentary Heritage.* Maryknoll, NY: Orbis, 1992.

O'Reilly, Kenneth. "The FBI and the Civil Rights Movement During the Kennedy Years— From the Freedom Rides to Albany." *Journal of Southern History* 54 (1988) 201–32.

"Operation Enduring Freedom." *Wikipedia.* Accessed January 26, 2008.

Parham, Sarah E. *The Life of Charles F. Parham: Founder of the Apostolic Faith Movement.* The Higher Christian Life. New York: Garland, 1985.

Pinn, Anthony B. *The Black Church in the Post–Civil Rights Era.* Maryknoll, NY: Orbis, 2002.

Piven, Frances Fox, and Richard A. Cloward. *Poor People's Movements: Why They Succeed and How They Fail.* New York: Vintage, 1979.

Raffacle, Martha. "Sixty-one Incumbents Face Primary Challenge." *Lancaster New Era,* April 11, 2006.

Rawls, John. *Collected Papers.* Edited by Samuel Freeman. Cambridge: Harvard University Press, 1999.

———. *A Theory of Justice.* Cambridge: Belknap Press of Harvard University Press, 1971.

"Rock the Vote." Accessed February 5, 2008. Online: http://www.rockthevote.com/cenorship/cen_index.php.

Rosenbaum, David E. "It's the Economy Again, as Democrats Attack the 'Contract with America.'" *New York Times,* November 1, 1994.

Rutenberg, Jim. "War Critics See New Resistance by Bush." *The New York Times,* December 26, 2006.

Saramago, José. *Seeing.* Translated by Margaret Jull Costa. Orlando: Harcourt, 2006.

Sartre, Jean-Paul. "Elections: A Trap for Fools." In *Life/Situations: Essays Written and Spoken,* 198–210. New York: Pantheon, 1977.

Schaumburger, M. M. *See* United States Bureau of Investigation.

Schier, Steven E. *You Call This an Election?: America's Peculiar Democracy.* Washington DC: Georgetown University Press, 2003.

Second Vatican Council. *Gaudium et Spes: Pastoral Constitution on the Church in the Modern World.* In *Catholic Social Thought: The Documentary Heritage,* edited by David J. O'Brien and Thomas A. Shannon, 163–237. Maryknoll, NY: Orbis, 1992.

Shuman, Joel. "Pentecost and the End of Patriotism: A Call for the Restoration of Pacifism among Pentecostal Christians." *Journal of Pentecostal Theology* 9 (1996) 70–96.

Smyth, Julie Carr. "Voting Machine Controversy." *Cleveland Plain Dealer,* August 28, 2003.

Stout, Jeffrey. *Democracy and Tradition.* Princeton: Princeton University Press, 2004.

Strayer, James. *On the Medieval Origins of the Modern State.* Princeton: Princeton University Press, 1970.

Tilly, Charles. *Coercion, Capital, and European States: AD 90–1992.* Revised paperback edition. Studies in Social Discontinuity. Cambridge, MA: Blackwell, 1993.

———. "Reflections on the History of European State-Making." In *The Formation of National States in Western Europe,* edited by Charles Tilly, 601–38. Studies in Political Development. Princeton: Princeton University Press, 1975.

———. "War Making and State Making as Organized Crime." In *Bringing the State Back In,* edited by Peter Evans, et al., 169–87. Cambridge: Cambridge University Press, 1985.

Toner, Robin. "A Loud Message for Bush." *New York Times,* November 8, 2006.

————. "To Democrats Hungry for Senate, a Pennsylvania Seat Looks Ripe." *New York Times*, March 5, 2006.

United States Bureau of Investigation. Agent M. M. Schaumburger to Bureau of Investigation, September 24, 1917, Old German case file 144128, Record Group 65. Investigation Case Files of the Bureau of Investigation, National Archives.

United States Commission on Presidential Debates. *The Third Bush-Kerry Debate*. Transcript of third candidates' debate between President George W. Bush and Senator John F. Kerry. Bob Schieffer, moderator. Arizona State University, Tempe, Arizona, October 13, 2004. Accessed February 4, 2008. Online: http://www.debates .org/pages/trans2004d.html.

United States Conference of Catholic Bishops. *Economic Justice for All*. In *Catholic Social Thought: The Documentary Heritage*, edited by David J. O'Brien and Thomas A. Shannon, 572–580. Maryknoll, NY: Orbis, 1992.

————. "Faithful Citizenship: A Call to Political Responsibility." Accessed February 5, 2008. Online: http://www.usccb.org/faithfulcitizenship/FCStatement.pdf.

United States Congress. House. Judiciary Committee. *Preserving Democracy: What Went Wrong in Ohio?* Democratic Staff. 108th Cong., 2d sess., December 8, 2004.

Urbina, Ian. "Democrats Fear Disillusionment in Black Voters." *New York Times*, October 27, 2006.

Urbina, Ian, and Christopher Drew. "Experts Concerned as Ballot Problems Persist." *New York Times*, December 26, 2006.

VandeHei, Jim. "Events Forcing Abortion Issue on Kerry." *Washington Post*, June 3, 2004, A6. Accessed February 4, 2008. Online: http://www.washingtonpost.com/wp-dyn/ articles/A11083-2004Jun2.html.

Villafañe, Eldin. *The Liberating Spirit: Toward an Hispanic American Pentecostal Social Ethic* Grand Rapids: Eerdmans, 1993.

Volf, Miroslav. *Exclusion and Embrace: A Theological Exploration of Identity, Otherness, and Reconciliation*. Nashville: Abingdon, 1996.

Wacker, Grant. *Heaven Below: Early Pentecostals and American Culture*. Cambridge: Harvard University Press, 2001.

Walters, Ronald W. *Freedom Is Not Enough: Black Voters, Black Candidates, and American Presidential Politics*. Lanham, MD: Rowan and Littlefield, 2005.

Walzer, Michael. *Just and Unjust Wars: A Moral Argument with Historical Illustrations*. 4th edition. New York: Basic, 2006.

Wenger, J. C. "Nonresistant and Nonpolitical." *Gospel Herald*, March 15, 1966. Accessed February 1, 2006, Online: http://www.bibleviews.com/nonpolitics.html.

Whitmore, Todd D. "In the Mission or On the Margins? A White Paper on the Teaching Catholic Social Teaching Project." *Current Issues in Catholic Higher Education* 22 (2002) 73–86.

————. "Teaching and Living Practical Reasoning: The Role of Catholic Social Thought in a Catholic University Curriculum." *Journal of Peace and Justice Studies* 11 (2001) 1–36.

————. "The Reception of Catholic Approaches to Peace and War in the United States." In *Modern Catholic Social Teaching: Commentaries and Interpretations*, edited by Kenneth R. Himes, 493–521. Washington DC: Georgetown University Press, 2005.

————. "What Would John Courtney Murray Say? On Abortion and Euthanasia." *Commonweal*, October 7, 1994, 16–22.

Wilgoren, Jodi. "The 2004 Campaign: The Former Governor; Dean Wants Party Leader to Slow Rivals' Attacks." *New York Times*, December 29, 2003. Accessed January 26, 2008. Online: http://query.nytimes.com/gst/fullpage.html?res=9C03EED7123EF93 AA15751C1A9659C8B63.

Wilson, Patricia. "Kerry: Still Would Have Approved Force for Iraq." Reuters, August 9, 2004. No pages. Accessed February 5, 2008. Online: http://news.myway.com/top/ article/id/381249%7Ctop%7C08-09-2004::17:46%7Creuters.html.

Wolin, Sheldon S. Occasional Papers. New York: New York University, Department of Political Science, 1990.

———. "Democracy and the Welfare State: The Political and Theoretical Connections between Staatsräson and Wohlfahrtsstaatsräson." *Political Theory* 15 (1987) 467–500.

———. "Democracy: Electoral and Athenian." *PS: Political Science and Politics* 26 (1993): 475–77.

———. *Politics and Vision: Continuity and Innovation in Western Political Thought.* Expanded edition. Princeton: Princeton University Press, 2004.

Women's Voices—Women's Vote. "Mission Statement." Accessed December 27, 2006. Online: http://www.wvwv.org/aboutwvwv/index.cfm?id=1.

Woodward, Kenneth L. "Catholics, Politics & Abortion." *Commonweal*, September 24, 2004.

Yoder, John Howard. *Body Politics: Five Practices of the Christian Community before the Watching World.* Scottdale, PA: Herald, 2001.

———. "Christ, the Hope of the World." In *The Royal Priesthood*, edited by Michael Cartwright, 194–218. Grand Rapids: Eerdmans, 1994.

———. "Civil Religion in America." In *The Priestly Kingdom: Social Ethics as Gospel*, 172–96. Notre Dame: University of Notre Dame Press, 1984.

———. "The Christian Case for Democracy." In *The Priestly Kingdom: Social Ethics as Gospel* 151–71. Notre Dame: University of Notre Dame Press, 1984.

———. *The Christian Witness to the State.* Scottdale: Herald, 2002.

———. *For the Nations: Essays Evangelical and Public.* Grand Rapids: Eerdmans, 1997.

———. Foreword to *Pentecostal Pacifism: The Origin, Development, and Rejection of Pacific Beliefs among Pentecostals*, Jay Beaman, iii–v. Hillsboro, KS: Center for Mennonite Brethren Studies, 1989.

———. "The Imperative of Christian Unity." In *The Royal Priesthood*, edited by Michael Cartwright, 289–99. Grand Rapids: Eerdmans, 1994.

———. "The Hermeneutics of Peoplehood." In *The Priestly Kingdom: Social Ethics as Gospel*, 15–45. Notre Dame: University of Notre Dame Press, 1984.

———. *Karl Barth and the Problem of War.* Studies in Christian Ethics Series. Nashville: Abingdon, 1970.

———. "The Kingdom as Social Ethic." In *The Priestly Kingdom*, 80–101. Notre Dame: University of Notre Dame Press, 1984.

———. "The National Ritual: Biblical Realism and the Elections." *Sojourners* 5 (1976) 29–30.

———. *The Priestly Kingdom: Social Ethics as Gospel.* Notre Dame: University of Notre Dame Press, 1984.

———. "Response of an Amateur Historian and a Religious Citizen." *The Journal of Law and Religion* 7 (1989) 415–32.

―――. *The Royal Priesthood: Essays Ecclesiological and Ecumenical.* Edited with an introduction by Michael G. Cartwright. Grand Rapids: Eerdmans, 1994.

―――. "Sacrament as Social Process: Christ the Transformer of Culture." In *The Royal Priesthood*, edited by Michael Cartwright, 359–73. Grand Rapids: Eerdmans, 1994.

Yoder, Nathan, and Carol A. Scheppard, editors. *Exiles in the Empire: Believers Church Perspectives on Politics.* Kitchener, Ontario: Pandora, 2006.

Young, Andrew. *An Easy Burden: The Civil Rights Movement and the Transformation of America.* New York: Harper Collins, 1996.

Zeleny, Jeff, and Megan Thee. "Exit Polls Show Independents, Citing War, Favored Democrats." *New York Times*, November 8, 2006.

Zinn, Howard. *A People's History of the United States 1492–Present.* Revised and updated edition. New York: HarperPerennial, 1995.

―――. *SNCC: The New Abolitionists.* Cambridge, MA: South End, 2002.

Contributors

John D. Roth teaches history at Goshen College, where he also serves as director of the Mennonite Historical Library and editor of the *Mennonite Quarterly Review*. In addition to numerous articles, Roth has written *Choosing Against War: A Christian View, Beliefs: Mennonite Faith and Practice*, and *Stories: How Mennonites Came to Be*. He is coeditor of *A Companion to Anabaptism and Spiritualism, 1521–1700*.

Andy Alexis-Baker graduated from Associated Mennonite Biblical Seminary in 2007 with an MA in theology and ethics. His master's thesis discussed peace and economics in the pre-Constantinian catechumenate in North Africa. Alexis-Baker has published articles in the Conrad Grebel Review and in the Ellul Forum. He plans to pursue a doctorate in patristics.

Nekeisha Alexis-Baker is originally from Trinidad but has spent much of her life in New York City. Since 2002 she has been involved in organizing conferences with Jesus Radicals on Christianity and anarchism. Alexis-Baker studied Africana Studies at New York University and is currently a graduate student in theology and ethics at Associated Mennonite Biblical Seminary.

G. Scott Becker died from cancer on September 13, 2007, in Pasadena, California, while this book was still in production. He was an ordained Baptist minister and a doctoral candidate in Christian ethics at Fuller Theological Seminary. He served as an adjunct instructor at Fuller and also at the Claremont School of Theology.

Michael Degan has been as an editor for Herald Press, the book division of Mennonite Publishing Network, since 2004. He previously worked as a writer and editor at newspapers and magazines around Philadelphia. Degan is a member of Forest Hills Mennonite Church in Leola, Pennsylvania.

Todd David Whitmore is Associate Professor of Christian ethics in the Department of Theology at the University of Notre Dame. He also serves as the director of the University's Program in Catholic Social Tradition. He has written widely on Catholic social teaching. His current research takes him to northern Uganda, where he is doing fieldwork in camps for internally displaced people.

Paul Alexander serves as Professor of Theology and Ethics, and as Director of the Doctor of Ministry Program in the Haggard Graduate School of Theology at Azusa Pacific University. He is also an Assemblies of God minister and the cofounder of the Pentecostal Charismatic Peace Fellowship (http://www.pcpf.org).

Tato Sumantri is a marketing assistant at Wipf and Stock Publishers. He is also a member of Church of the Servant King, an intentional and worshiping community that meets as a house church in Eugene, Oregon. Sumantri is husband of Sheri Winchell and father to daughter Raydeen and son Joshua. Born in Bellefonte, Pennyslvania, Sumantri grew up moving about before joining Church of the Servant King in Gardena, California. He and his family moved to Eugene to partner with Jon and Cindy Stock in helping to begin a house church and intentional community there.

Ted Lewis is an acquisitions editor for Wipf and Stock Publishers, and he manages the Restorative Justice Program at Community Mediation Services. He also provides mediation work for the Pacific Northwest Mennonite Conference. Ted lives with his wife, Nancy (and daughters Elie and Clarity), and is part of Church of the Servant King.